DENNIS SAYLOR

# *The*
# Ceremonies of Judaism

By ABRAHAM Z. IDELSOHN

*Professor of Jewish Music and Liturgy*
*Hebrew Union College*

## National Federation of Temple Brotherhoods
### CINCINNATI
1930

PRINTED IN U. S. A.

 2

# PREFACE

THE "Ceremonies of Judaism" was first written for and published in the Temple Brotherhood Monthly (The Jewish Layman), 1928-1929, in nine lessons. The first publication in book form was enlarged by the description of mourning ceremonies and by an introductory note on Sabbath. This present (second) edition includes two additional chapters: "Ceremonial Objects in the Synagogue" and "Prayer and Song," besides the insertion in Chapter II of the statement on the Dietary Laws.

In this presentation of the "Ceremonies of Judaism," the author does not enter into a scientific dissertation of the origins and history of the various practices; but offers a popular illustrated description, intended to familiarize the reader with the essential customs of the Jewish religion.

This publication is but a part of the program of the National Federation of Temple Brotherhoods to supply the means for spreading amongst our laity a greater knowledge of matters Jewish. The fact that the first printing of the "Ceremonies of Judaism" was exhausted within nine months after its appearance is but further proof that our laymen to-day are seeking knowledge about their faith, which only places the greater responsibility on the leaders of Israel to supply the material and aid in the direction of its study.

NATIONAL FEDERATION OF TEMPLE BROTHERHOODS.

# Contents

Introduction

## I. Sabbath and Festivals

## II. Daily Ceremonies in Home and Synagogue

v

## III. Ceremonial Objects in the Synagogue

## IV. Prayer and Song
### (Pages 93 to 115)

## V. Ceremonies for Special Occasions in the Life of the Individual

# INTRODUCTION

EVERY religion has ceremonies. Indeed there can be no creed without its forms, because a faith manifests itself through prayer and action, both of which gradually crystalise into rites, genuinely expressive of a certain group's thoughts, dreams, manner of life, and history. The time of worship and the place of worship become established. The manner of voicing and symbolizing ideas, takes definite shape. In the course of time, certain determining events in the life of the adherents of a religion, find permanent place in the religious calendar. Thus ceremonies deal at once with the profoundest ideals and the minutest habits of daily life. Only those people can appreciate them who understand the thought, the belief, the hope, or the incident for which they stand. They can be "lifeless" and "meaningless" only to those who see them with eyes but not with heart or head.

As a religion develops, changing certain attitudes, and reaching toward loftier concepts, its followers sometimes abandon the ceremonies that symbolize the out-grown notions. But mostly these customs live on, after their content is changed into a loftier ideal, reflecting a higher religious conception.

In its long history Judaism has naturally evolved a unique expression of itself, in its ceremonies.

# 1

# THE SABBATH, THE FESTIVALS AND COMMEMORATIVE DAYS

*"Remember the Sabbath Day to keep it holy."*
*These festive and commemorative days*
*are given unto Israel to remind*
*him of his past and to*
*strengthen his faith.*

# *S*ABBATH

THE distinguishing of the seventh day of the week is very old. The Babylonians observed the seventh, fourteenth, twenty-first, and twenty-eighth days of two months during the year. These days were called "Days of Penitence." On them, the leaders of the people were not allowed to eat meat, to drink certain beverages, to wear fine clothes, or to ride in fine carriages. In addition they were forbidden to work. The Semitic tribes considered the seventh day an ill-omened one on which no task could be successful.

In Israel, the observance of the seventh day became a permanent weekly institution. The day was designated *Sabbath* (cessation of work); and was ordained not only for the leaders but for the entire people, for even the slaves and the beasts of burden. Moreover, Israel changed the thought back of the day from the ominous to the happy; and substituted for the pagan notion of a day on which the gods are angry, the loftier idea that God—finishing the world on this day, and being satisfied with His creation—sanctified and blessed the day as one of rest and joy, (Genesis 2:3). In the fourth commandment (Exodus 20:8-11), the law became binding for the entire household of Israel. The inclusion of the Sabbath in the Ten Commandments gives evidence of the importance with which the institution was regarded.

The observance of the Sabbath, as it is laid down in the Bible, consisted in refraining from labour. We read of noth-

3

ing else then prescribed for that day. Little by little the spiritual leaders, realizing the great value of a resting day for the spiritual elevation of a people, instituted regular assemblage, at which portions of the Pentateuch and Prophets were read and explained. Thus the day was utilized to instruct the people in their Holy Scriptures. In addition, a public service was developed, consisting of prayers and hymns chanted by the congregation and the reader. This ritual was established centuries before the destruction of the Second Temple.

In the course of the generations, the sanctity of the Sabbath became so deeply rooted in the soul of the Jewish people that no force could destroy it. Neither the Greeks nor the Romans succeeded in preventing Sabbath observance, through their many prohibitions, or under threat of the penalty of death. The Jew felt instinctively that the Sabbath is one of the foundations of his Jewish life. On this day he tried to forget all his worries, and to devote himself entirely to his spiritual elevation, to bodily relaxation and joy. During the long dark period of the Middle Ages, the Sabbath was one of the high spots which kept Israel alive—a beam of light in the thick darkness. Hence there arose the proverb: Israel could not exist without the Sabbath.

Israel's conception was: The Sabbath is given to you for your benefit; not that you should suffer on account of it. To carry out this principle, the law provided for the nullification of any or all prohibitions, in a question of saving one's life, or for the sick. No mourning nor fasting nor sadness are permitted on this day.

Sabbath abstinence from work was constantly being defined in Jewish law and practice. But the idea of what constitutes labour, changes in the course of time. Certain of the old prohibitions thus lose significance and are ignored.

4

BLESSING
THE
SABBATH
LIGHTS

*Boris Schatz*

The Sabbath provides for both spirit and body. It is a means by which the Jew is given entirely to his faith, to his people, and to his family. The way in which the Jewish people observed the Sabbath, changed but little (until modern times) in the last eighteen centuries.

### THE EVE OF SABBATH

On Friday morning, preparations started: the making of the special food; the cleaning of the house. From oldest times, the Jews have celebrated their festivals with special lights. The obligation to kindle the Sabbath lights rested on the women. Thus, on Friday evening before sunset, the wife lights the candles (minimum two), or kindles the Sabbath oil-lamp, and recites a special benediction. Many artistic forms of Sabbath lamps have been created. They are usually pendant metal bowls to contain the oil, with small projecting

M. *Oppenheim*

FRIDAY EVENING BLESSING BY THE FATHER

spouts to hold the tapers, or candelabras with three or more arms. Many use ornamented silver, copper or brass candlesticks.

After the kindling of the lights, in the old homes, the table is set for the evening meal; and the women attire themselves in Sabbath garments. Meanwhile the male members of the family are in the Synagogue "to receive the Sabbath."

This special service is called *Kabbalath Shabbath,* the receiving of Queen Sabbath. The ritual consists of seven Psalms and a hymn "Lechah dodi," followed by the regular evening service with some special insertions. Distinctive tunes for this service were created in the course of centuries, notably those for "Lechah dodi" (about two thousand melodies!) This number of compositions for a single poem is unique in musical literature.

When the father of the household returns home from the Synagogue, he blesses his wife and children. Then the family sings *Shalom Alechem,* a hymn built on a statement in the Talmud that two angels of peace accompany each man home from the Synagogue, and remain with him and his family all the Sabbath day. The father recites Proverbs 31: 10-31, that beautiful eulogy of woman. Then the family is seated at table and the father recites the Sanctification *(Kiddush)* over bread and wine (fermented or unfermented). In the spirit of home celebration of the Sabbath, certain chosen articles of food came to be associated with the day, and to be distinctive of it. When a famous Rabbi was once asked by a Roman noble, how it was that the Jewish Sabbath food is supposed to be so tasty, the Rabbi replied: We have a certain spice which we put into our food. This spice is called "The Observance of the Sabbath." Sabbath bread, called *Challah,* usually a twisted white loaf, was always prepared and baked at home. The first dish served was fish. The use of fish for Sabbath is very old. We find it mentioned in Nehemiah 13:16. Later a symbolic meaning was attached to it. Israel was compared to fish that persist though persecuted. The next dish was soup with noodles, *Lokshen,* and the third, *Tzimmes* (carrots and potatoes mixed with sugar and oil or meat fat).

Between the courses, table songs—*Zemiroth* are sung. The meal concludes with the singing of *Shir Hamaaloth* (Psalm 126) and the chanting of Grace—*Benshen* (the Latin "Benedictio" Germanized). The custom of singing table-songs, *Zemiroth,* dates back to long before the destruction of the Second Temple. During the course of twenty centuries, these songs added light and joy to the Jewish soul on Sabbath. A rich collection of songs was created, mostly in Hebrew, the content of which is the glorification of the Sabbath, of the Torah and of Israel's spiritual heritage. In recent years several of them have been translated into English. *Zemiroth* singing is a custom that cannot be allowed to die, for it enriches our soul with its gentle joyous piety.

In the modern homes in this country, the participation of women in all the religious functions, has somewhat shifted the order of the ritual. For instance, the kindling of the Sabbath candles is usually done at the Sabbath table, in the presence of the united family. After the meal, men and women together attend the religious service. Many congregations have abandoned the *Kabbalath Shabbath* service for the late after-supper worship. This service, attended by men and women, young and old, observed in the leisure after the evening meal, has proved of great religious influence.

### SATURDAY

On Saturday morning there are Synagogue services in which the reading of the Pentateuch *(Torah)* and Prophets *(Haftarah)* occupies the central place. The *Torah* is read from a Scroll *(Sefer-Torah),* made of parchment upon which the writing is done by hand, as in ancient times. (See page 85). In the Reform Synagogue, the Hegiographa is also read as Haftarah.

BESAMIM-BOX
*(H. U. C. Museum)*

After the service is over the family takes the main meal, at which a special dish is served, called Chalent, from the French "chaleur": warmth, warm food. Since no cooking or fire-making was permissible on Sabbath, people used to prepare the Sabbath meal on Friday, and set it into an oven kept hot with glowing coals. The *Chalent* consists of a meat soup with barley and potatoes, and of the famous *Kugel* (German, meaning "Ball"), that is, noodle or bread pudding. *Zemiroth* are sung and the meal is concluded with the singing of *Shir Hamaaloth* and the chanting of grace.

After the meal it was customary for the father to examine his sons in their Jewish studies and to repeat with them the weekly portion of the Pentateuch, chanted according to the *Neginoth* called *Trop* (from the Latin *tropus*). This chant, part of the most genuine music of ancient Israel, the Reform Synagogue has unfortunately abolished. For the women a special literature was created in Yiddish: popular presentations of Midrashic and ethical literature. It was their only instruction, which they read with great interest every Saturday afternoon. These old Jewish homes presented an inspiring picture, Saturday afternoon—every member of the family either reading or studying.

Sabbath afternoon the people reassembled in the Syna-

M. *Oppenheim*

SABBATH AFTERNOON

gogue where, often, a popular lecturer or preacher (*Maggid*) would hold discourse on a religio-ethical theme, after which the *Minchah* service was read. Upon the return home, the "third meal" (*Shalosh Seudoth*) was served.

### The Outgoing of Sabbath

At sunset, men re-assembled in the unlighted Synagogue, where the congregation would chant Psalms in responsive form. The yearning note of the melody, together with the semi-darkness of the Synagogue, created a mysterious atmosphere, reminiscent of one's feelings at the departure of a dear friend. Then the evening service *(Maarib)* was intoned in the week-day tune. At the conclusion of it, either the *Chazzan* or the *Shammash* kindled the *Habdalah* candle and, over the wine, chanted the *Habdalah* (Separation) benediction; that is, the "Separation" between the Sabbath and the week-days, between the sacred and the profane. This ceremony was then repeated by each householder at his home, where in addition, a benediction over spices was recited. The spices were kept in a special box artistically worked in gold, silver or other metal, called *Besamin*-box. This custom was introduced with the purpose of delighting the yearning spirit at the moment when the beloved Sabbath is departing. Much artistry is displayed also in the making of the wax *"Habdalah"* candles.

The *Habdalah* ceremony included a custom of turning one's hands toward the light of the candle and of reciting a benediction for the creation of artificial light, when the spiritual light, Sabbath, is leaving us.

Before the kindling of the light at the outgoing of Sabbath, the women used to chant in Yiddish *"Got Fun Avrohom,"* a prayer that the coming week be a happy and prosperous one.

*H. Struck*

HABDALAH

# $\gamma$OMIM $\mathcal{N}$ORAIM

## (The High Holidays)

THE season of the High Holidays begins, in the Ortho-dox congregations, with *Elul,* the month before *Rosh Hashanah.* Throughout the month, every day after the morning service, the *Shofar* is blown (*Tekiah-Shevarim-Teruah-Tekiah*) to prepare the people for the coming Days of Awe (*Yomim Noraim*). In Oriental congregations, it is customary, during the entire month, to rise early and, before sunrise, to recite supplications (*Selichoth*). European Jews observe this custom for only a few days.

### Rosh Hashanah

The Jewish religious year starts with the first day of the Jewish month *Tishri,* which as a rule falls between the middle of September and the beginning of October. In Bible times, the political year in Israel started with the Spring month *Nissan;* and *Tishri* is recorded in the Bible as the seventh month. Leviticus 23:24 says: "In the seventh month, in the first day of the month, shall be a solemn rest unto you, a memorial proclaimed with the blast of horns, a holy convocation." The Bible does not explain what is meant by memorial, and what the contents of that holiday were. In Numbers 29:1-6 the day is called a day of the blowing of the horn. We presume that since the Jewish religious calendar started with the month of *Tishri,* the idea of the "day of blowing of the horn" can be understood as the announcement of the New Year. The religious idea attached to the day was that of memorial, that is, on that day God considers every individ-

12

ual in the world, carefully weighing the merits and short-comings of his deeds. Later the idea of Judgment was increasingly emphasized, until *Rosh Hashanah* became a day of awe. On it each person sought to set himself right before God. If God is the Judge in whose hand is life and death, He is thus the Ruler of the world. Therefore much stress was laid upon the proclamation of God as the only Ruler of the world—an idea which was worked out in most beautiful language and style in the Hebrew prayers for the day.

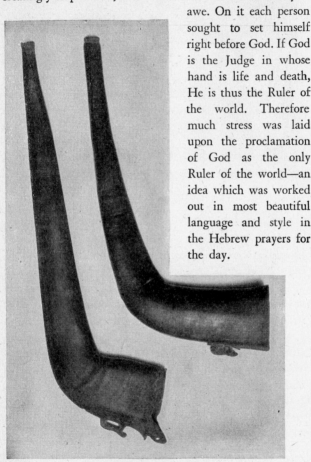

SHOFAROTH (H. U. C. Museum)

THE SHOFAR BLOWER

*Rosh Hashanah* is one of those Jewish holidays in which the idea of the individual is emphasized. As Ruler and Judge, God makes no distinction between nations and religious groups. On that day He considers every human being regardless of his nationality. *Rosh Hashanah* is bound to neither nation nor locality.

The idea of the Day of Judgment produced a special liturgy and special customs. The nucleus of this liturgy was created already at the time when the Second Temple still existed in Jerusalem.

A mystic significance was attached to the custom of Blowing the Shofar. In ancient times the blasts of the horn were believed to have the power of driving away evil spirits. To convert this pagan notion into a higher religious idea, the Jewish sages said that the *Shofar* is blown to remind us of the intended sacrifice of Isaac, for—according to tradition—

14

Abraham attempted to sacrifice Isaac on that very day on the spot where the Jerusalem Temple was later erected. Since by the command of God, a ram was substituted for Isaac (see Genesis, 22), the sages explained that the blowing of a ram's horn would remind us of God's providence. Later the Jewish philosophers Saadia and Maimonides introduced the still loftier concept that the sound of the *Shofar* has the unique quality of penetrating into the human soul and causing the heart to tremble. The blowing of the *Shofar* in the service was, according to Rabbinic prescription, divided into four sections, totaling one hundred calls. Three sections have thirty calls each, and the fourth has ten calls. The sounds of the *Shofar* are these: 1. *Tekiah,* one sustained tone ending abruptly on the fourth or fifth note above the sustained tone; 2. *Shevarim,* three groups of two notes each, each making the step of a fourth or fifth; 3. *Teruah,* nine very short disconnected (staccato) notes, or a tremulo on one tone. After the blowing of these three different calls, the *Tekiah* is repeated. Each of these calls irrespective of the number of its tones, was considered a unit (one blast). The calls are executed according to this scheme: The group *Tekiah-Shevarim-Teruah-Tekiah* is rendered three times (total, twelve calls); then the group *Tekiah-Shevarim-Tekiah* three times

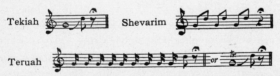

(nine calls); and finally *Tekiah-Teruah-Tekiah* thrice (nine calls). The sum of these three groups is thirty. This succession of thirty calls, blown three times, amounts to ninety. To complete the hundred, a final group of ten is added in the order: 1. *Tekiah-Shevarim-Teruah-Tekiah;* 2. *Tekiah-Sheva-rim-Tekiah;* 3. *Tekiah-Teruah-Tekiah.* The last *Tekiah* of each of the four sections is prolonged and is called *Tekiah gedolah*—The big *Tekiah.*

For the construction of a *Shofar,* a ram's horn is first softened by boiling; then scraped inside, that its hollow may be smooth; and finally well hardened that it may be vibrant. Frequently it is beautified with surface carvings. At best, it can produce but a few tones—these not of musical quality but of the nature of signals.

No member of the Jewish household, man or woman, was permitted to taste of food at noon on *Rosh Hashanah,* unless he had heard the *Shofar.* For people confined to their beds, the *Shofar* was carried to the sick room and blown in private houses. In case *Rosh Hashanah* falls on Sabbath the blowing of the *Shofar* is omitted in the Orthodox Synagogue, because it is considered labour.

For two days' celebration of Rosh Hashanah, see a later treatment on Calendar.

The special greeting of Jew to Jew on Rosh Hashanah is the formula: "May you be inscribed for a good year" (*Leshonoh tovoh tikosev,* plural: *tikosevu*).

Special items of diet became associated with the *Rosh Hashanah* meal. Honey was set onto the table, and the bread was dipped into it, while the head of the house pronounced the words: "May it be His will that this year be a sweet one." The special loaves of white bread were formed round and smooth, as a symbol of the desire that the year too be smooth and round.

In about the tenth or eleventh century, the custom of *Tashlich* arose. On the first day of *Rosh Hashanah* after the afternoon service, the congregation would go to the edge of

*Stryowiski in Jew. Encyc. Vol. XII*

TASHLICH CEREMONY IN GALICIA

a river, lake, sea or any flowing water—there to recite a ritual concluding: "May God cast our sins into the depths of the sea." The men would shake the ends of their coats and their sleeves, as though brushing off their sins. The name of the ceremony, *Tashlich,* means "casting off." The custom survives to this day in Orthodox circles, despite the opposition of many prominent rabbis.

## THE FAST OF GEDALIA

commemorates a historical event mentioned in II Kings 25:22-25. Gedalia had been appointed Governor of Palestine after the destruction of the First Temple; but on the day following *Rosh Hashanah* he was killed; and with him the independence of the Jewish people was wiped out. Hence on the day succeeding *Rosh Hashanah,* pious Jews fast and hold

17

a special service, the distinctive prayers of which are supplications *(Selichoth)*.

## THE TEN DAYS OF PENITENCE

The period from the first day of *Rosh Hashanah* until *Yom Kippur* (which falls on the tenth of *Tishri*) is called the Ten Days of Penitence *(Asereth Yemey Teshuvah)*. During this period pious Jews used to fast every day until sunset. Long before sunrise every night they gathered (and many Orthodox Jews still gather) for special supplications *(Selichoth)*.

On the day before *Yom Kippur,* the custom called *Kapporos* (ransom) was observed. The idea back of this custom is very old. In ancient times people sacrificed animals, believing that instead of offering their own bodies, they were substituting animals. During the time of the Temple, on every *Yom Kippur* a scape-goat *(Azazel)* was sent from the Temple into the desert, to carry away the sins of the people (Leviticus 16:22). After the destruction of the Second Temple, it was impossible to continue the sending of a goat; and the people felt that they had no means of offering a ransom. They created a substitute in the form of *Kapporos*. They chose for their ransom a fowl, usually a chicken, upon the head of which each person laid his sins; and, while swinging the chicken above his head three times, he recited: "The chicken is my substitute and my ransom, and shall be killed that I may survive for a long and peaceful life." White chickens were perferable because white symbolized purity and innocence. Women would select hens, and men roosters. After the ceremony, the fowl was killed and cooked, and served at the meal on the Eve of *Yom Kippur*. If lack of sufficient funds prevented the purchase of fowl, a few

18

coins given to charity would constitute a substitute atone-ment. The formula of the recitation was then changed thus: "The coin is my substitute and my ransom and shall be given for charity that I may survive," etc. In spite of the strong opposition of many famous rabbis throughout the centuries, this custom still survives.

An hour before sunset on the Eve of *Yom Kippur*, Jews partake of the *Seudah Hammafseketh* (cessation-meal), that is the end of all eating until about an hour after sunset of the following day. The meal has special dishes associated with it. There are breads formed in the shape of ladders, as a symbol that our prayers should ascend. *Kreplach*, small pieces of noodle-dough folded in triangular form and stuffed with ground meat, are served in the soup.

As the day before *Yom Kippur* is considered a festival, candles are lit at the cessation meal, and the benediction

*L. Pilichowski*

SCH'MA YISROEL

19

recited as on the eve of the festivals. After the meal, long candles are lit, intended to last throughout the twenty-four hours. In days when each household prepared its own candles much care and ingenuity were expended in moulding and braiding the *Yom Kippur* candles.

After the meal, it was customary for the father to bless the children, his wife, and all the members of his household. Then the family (excluding babies) would prepare itself to go to the Synagogue. All would walk to the Synagogue in stockings or slippers, as a symbol of humility and suffering.

Before the beginning of the service, which started before sunset, each Jew sought forgiveness of anyone whom he had wronged, for Jewish doctrine teaches that the Day of Atonement does not atone for wrongs done to one's neighbor, unless the neighbor's forgiveness be obtained; and that there is no atonement before God until atonement before man be accomplished.

At the entrance of the Synagogue, there were plates for charity *(Kaaroth);* and every one would drop into them as much as he was able to give.

## The Eve of Yom Kippur

Before the *Kol Nidre* service started every man put on a white robe called *Kittl,* and wrapped himself in the *Tallith.* These two garments the men wore all through the fast day. The *Kittl* was used not only for *Yom Kippur,* but also for the Passover *Seder* and for burial. Its use on *Yom Kippur* was intended as a reminder of death. At the opening of the service the curtains of the Ark are drawn, the Scrolls are taken out, and the *Chazzan* sings that wonderful, awesome, inspiring tune *Kol Nidre,* from which the entire evening service takes its name.

## THE DAY OF ATONEMENT—YOM KIPPUR

In the religious calendar, *Yom Kippur* (Lev. 16:29-34) to the Jew is the most sacred of days, one devoted entirely to prayer and meditation. All the household of Israel refrains from physical work and enjoyment, and from nourishment. Even washing with soap is avoided by Jews of the old school. Many pious Jews used to remain in the Synagogue twenty-four hours standing on their feet, reading and praying without interruption. *Yom Kippur,* like *Rosh Hashanah,* is universalistic in appeal. The final service of *Yom Kippur* concludes with a prolonged call on the *Shofar: Tekiah-Shevarim-Teruah-Tekiah gedolah.* In some congregations only one *Tekiah* is blown.

At the end of the day, it is customary for one to greet the other with the wish: "A happy New Year, and a good sealing," that is the sealing of the divine decree concerning each life, for the period of the year just beginning.

After the service in the Orthodox Synagogue, the *Chazzan* recites *Habdalah* over wine. (For details of this ceremony, see the treatment on Sabbath ceremonies.) Every householder, on his return home, was accustomed to repeat the ceremony, after which he went into his yard and started building the *Succah,* in order to begin the New Year with some pious deed.

Then followed the *"Anbeissen,"* the breaking of the fast. Everyone was in high spirits, confident that a happy year had been granted him.

# *S*UCCOTH

## *(The Feast of Booths)*

**F**OUR days after *Yom Kippur,* on the fifteenth of *Tishri,*
begins *Succoth.* The name means booths. According to
Leviticus 23:42 the booth commemorates the life of the Israelites in the desert after leaving Egypt. The holiday was
called also the Harvest Festival because, according to the Bible (Deuteronomy 16:13-15) it was celebrated after the people
had finished their harvesting. The festival of *Succoth* lasts
eight successive days, seven of which are *Succoth* proper,
while the eighth is observed as a Concluding Festival called
*Shemini Atzereth.*

*Succoth* is designated as a festival of joy; and is distinguished by several colorful and meaningful customs. In the
first place, there is the *Succah,* a booth covered with green
branches completely severed from the trees. It must be not
less than seven fists (about four feet) in length and in
width, and not higher than twenty cubits (about 25 feet).
Inside, the *Succah* is decorated with fruits of different types.
This task is the obligation of the women.

In this *Succah* the men were obliged to take all their
meals; and they were commanded to dwell in it during the
week of the festival, unless forced indoors by rain or extreme
cold. Women were exempted from this obligation. Nevertheless, no woman ever took the liberty of eating elsewhere
than in the *Succah.* Happy hours were spent there during
the week, in song and rejoicing and also in study. Men
considered it a duty to read the Talmudic portions dealing

# Succoth—The Feast of Booths

M. Oppenheim

THE SUCCAH

with the laws and regulations of this festival.

During the Medieval ages, the *Succah* was interpreted as a symbol of simplicity, frailty, and humility. Rich and poor were urged to abandon their residence and to move to the booth. Its frailness stimulated them to think of life as a temporary sojourn and of prosperity and poverty as likewise temporary.

Next in importance to the *Succah* is the group of the Four Species: *Ethrog* (a citron); *Lulab* (a shoot of a palm tree in its folded state before the leaves are spread out); *Hadassah* (three twigs of myrtle); *Aravah* (two willow branches). These four species are mentioned already in the Pentateuch, Leviticus 23:40.

During the period of the Second Temple, the people with these four species in their hands used to march in procession around the altar singing: "I beseech Thee, O Lord, grant salvation; I beseech Thee, O Lord, grant prosperity." After the destruction of the Second Temple this custom was transplanted into the Synagogue, where it survives to the present day, under the name *Hakafoth* (circuits).

The three species are arranged in this way: a triple holder of braided palm leaves supports the *Lulab* in the center, the *Hadassah* to its right, and the *Aravah* to its left. The

23

*I. Kaufmann*

CHASSIDIC BOY HOLDING LULAB
AND ETHROG

*Ethrog* is kept separate. The origin of the use of these, we do not know with certainty. The rabbis devised an ethical interpretation, according to which the four species represent four types of men: the proud (*Lulab*), the humble (*Aravah*), the one with beautiful qualities, but without good deeds (*Hadassah*). The highest type, the one whose virtuous deeds have an influence upon others, the rabbis liken to the fine perfume of the *Ethrog*. The combining of these, symbolizes the brotherhood of the human race.

Jewish artistic instinct manifested itself in creating wonderful containers for the *Ethrog,* worked in gold, silver, or other metals. These gave expression to the devotion of the Jew to the religious ideals embodied in this symbol.

*Succoth* is designated in the Bible as the "Season of our rejoicing." Originally in Palestine, it marked a final Thanksgiving celebration after the completion of harvesting. Though conditions have changed, the expression is retained: "Season of our rejoicing." Indeed, for us today, there is the same vitality in the idea of humility expressed through the *Succah;*

24

in the significance ascribed to the four species; in the great principles of genuine thanksgiving.

The seventh day of *Succoth* is called *Hoshanah Rabbah* (the great salvation). According to old tradition the final sealing of the decree (see *Yom Kippur*) is not completed on *Yom Kippur* but on this day. Consequently, in addition to the *Succoth* significance, this day received a sanctity akin to the spirit of the High Holidays. During the night of this festival a watch takes place, on which a special ritual is recited. Its morning service was created of parts of the *Yom Kippur* prayers fused with parts of the *Succoth* service. It contains both supplications and the *Hallel*. After the reader and worshippers encircle the synagogue platform seven times with the four species in their hands, everybody lays aside the four species and takes a bunch of willows (called, in consequence, *Hoshanah*) with which he beats the bench

BLESSING OF THE LULAB AND ETHROG

or floor three times, while calling: "A voice proclaims good tidings." As a sign of reminiscence of the High Holidays, the *chazzan* wears the *Kittl* and sings many High Holiday tunes. At the meal, the "ladder" bread, *Kreplach* and honey are served.

On the eighth day, *Shemini Atzereth* (The eighth day of convocation), a special prayer is offered, called *Tefillath Geshem*—Prayer for rain. It was instituted in Palestine, where, after a half-year of drought, rain starts in Fall, and continues throughout the Winter until Spring. The solemnity of this prayer is expressed by the *chazzan's* wearing the *Kittl,* as well as by a special tune, "the Dew and Rain tune."

After the morning service, people take leave of the *Succah;* and all the fruit and decorations which adorned it are given to the children, or to charity.

## SIMCHATH TORAH

The evening of this day and the day following are called *Simchath Torah* (Rejoicing over the Law). This festival, though the latest instituted (about the ninth or the tenth century), has nonetheless achieved equal sanctity with those festivals dating from Biblical times. The underlying idea of it is unique. It is dissociated from any special locality and from all primitive religious conceptions. It voices the pure joy and love and sense of privilege which the Jew feels for being in possession of the *Torah.* On this day the annual cycle of weekly readings of the Pentateuch in the Synagogue is completed and immediately begun anew, as a symbol that the Jew should never finish reading the *Torah.* After the evening service, all the Scrolls are taken out of the Ark and a lighted candle placed in it to substitute the *Torahs*—symbol

THE PROCESSION WITH LULAB AND ETHROG

of light. The members of the congregation are honored with the privilege of carrying the Scrolls. They form a procession *(Hakafoth)*, with the *Chazzan* at the head, and encircle the synagogue auditorium seven times, chanting special hymns for the occasion, singing joyous religious folk songs, the texts of which deal with the *Torah*.

The children are encouraged to participate in the joyous celebration. They are presented with special paper flags, printed in Hebrew, with the words: "The crown of the *Torah.*" These and illuminated lanterns, they carry in lines following the procession *(Hakafoth)* of the adults. And they join the singing of their elders. The following day the same circuit is repeated.

During the reading of the last portion of the Pentateuch every member of the congregation is called upon to recite the benediction over the *Torah*. After every man has had an opportunity, all boys under thirteen are called in a group before the *Torah;* an adult recites the benediction with them, while covering them with his *Tallith*. The congregation then rises and recites Gen. 48:16.

A prominent member of the congregation is called upon to finish the Pentateuch. This man is called *Chathan Torah* —the bridegroom of the *Torah*. Special prayers are recited for him by the reader; and the congregation honors him by chanting aloud: *"Chazak, chazak venithchazak,"* "Be strong and fortified in your championing of the *Torah*."

Immediately after the *Torah* is concluded, another prominent member is invited to begin the new cycle of reading

HAKAFOTH OF SIMCHATH TORAH

with the opening section of the Pentateuch. He receives the title *Chathan Bereshith* — bridegroom of Genesis.

At the end of the service, the *Chathan Torah* usually invites the congregation to his home for a banquet, at which occasion the celebration of the day reaches its climax, through joyous *Simchath Torah* songs, and toasts of religious content.

# CHANUKAH

## (The Feast of Lights)

CHANUKAH commemorates the victory of an ideal over brutality, spiritual independence over despotism, light over darkness. A handful of Jews, conscious of the high value of their spiritual culture, their religion, dared open fight against the overwhelming power of the Syrian King, Antiochus Epiphanes, who aimed to crush their faith in the one God, and to suppress the ritual and ceremonies created by the Jewish people to give voice to its beliefs.

In the year 162 B. C. E. King Antiochus Epiphanes ordered that a pagan altar be set up in the Temple in Jerusalem and that sacrifices be offered to the Greek idol Zeus Olympus. After hard struggle and bitter battles, in which many Jewish heroes lost their lives on the battlefield, the pious ones under the leadership of Judas the Hasmonean, or Maccabeus, achieved victory after victory, until he reconquered Jerusalem, drove out the Syrians and their Jewish sympathizers, and purified the Temple from the Zeus cult.

This purification occurred on the 25th of the Jewish month *Kislev*. The altar was sanctified and dedicated anew, lamps and torches kindled as a symbol of spiritual light and freedom, and a celebration of eight days ordained, during which the illumination continued amid sacrifices and songs. This feast was decreed by Judas Maccabeus and the elders of Israel to be celebrated annually, and was called *Chanukah*— "Feast of Dedication," also "Festival of Lights." There is a Talmudic legend that all the oil in the Temple was polluted by the pagan worshippers, and that upon investigation only one cruse of consecrated oil was found by the Hasmoneans, untouched, sealed and hidden away. This cruse was used to illuminate the Temple. Its oil lasted, by miracle, for eight days.

The story of Chanukah has been preserved in the first four chapters of the first book of the Maccabees (in the Apocrypha) and in the "Scroll Antiochus" *(Megillath Antiochus),* printed in many Orthodox prayerbooks.

In the morning service of each of the eight days, "Hallel" (Psalms 113-118) is recited, a portion of the Pentateuch (Numbers 7) is read, also a paragraph briefly sketching the story of Chanukah. In the evenings oil lamps or waxen candles are lit. Originally these lights used to be set outdoors as a manifestation of the victory of light over darkness. But through fanatical Medieval oppression the Jews were forced to keep their lights indoors. They had to be content to set them in the windows. Originally big flames were kindled, but Medieval tyranny reduced them to tiny sparks. However, they were never extinguished by all the violent storms which raged against Judaism throughout the ages.

The lights are lit in the Synagogue as well as in each private home. Starting with one light on the first evening, the number is increased by one each evening, until on the eighth night there are eight lights. This progression is a symbol of Judaism's belief in the gradual constant increase of intellectual light and of the slow but steady victory of spiritual enlightenment. Lovingly and beautifully has Jewish art molded and ornamented the Chanukah lamp or candelabra.

At the kindling of the lights special benedictions are recited for the miracles which God showed to our forefathers at this season. Then the hymn *"Mooz tzur"* or "Rock of Ages," the English adaptation thereof, is sung, according

CHANUKAH LAMP—*Courtesy, A. M. Burd, Germantown, Pa.*
*Designed and made by Reuben Leaf, New York City.*

to a melody popular among the German Jews since the 16th century. Though the elements of this tune are German, the melody is not found in this form in the German folksong. While the lights burn, no work is permitted. Jews are accustomed to indulge in games and in the eating of *latkes* (pancakes). Children play with a revolving top or die, called *Dreidle* or *Trendle* (from the German *drehen*). This die has on its four sides Hebrew letters: נ, ג, ה, and ש which had a twofold meaning, the one in Hebrew: *nes gadol hayah sham* ("A great miracle happened there"), and the German one: *nichts, ganz, halb, stell* (nothing, all, half, put), indicating the gains and losses in the play. The children usually receive presents from their parents, relatives and friends ("*Chanukah Gelt*" or "*Chanukah Geshenk*").

31

With the strengthening of Jewish self-consciousness in the last few decades, Chanukah has assumed an importance in the Jewish calendar commensurate with its historical and religious significance. This festival buoys up the Jew's spirit that he may withstand the waves of assimilation; that his eyes may not be blinded by the gilded splendour of false gods; that, being a small minority in an overwhelming ma-

TRENDLE

jority, he be not made timid, that he may not underestimate his own spiritual culture in the face of that vast culture surrounding and engulfing him. Inspirited by the message of this festival the Jew must champion the truth of his religion, that which made the Maccabees conquer Syrianized Hellenism, and which, ever since, has kindled in the hearts of millions of the human race the eternal light of the Jewish faith.

# CHAMISHAH ASAR BISHVAT

THIS day occurs six weeks after Chanukah on the fifteenth of the Jewish month *Shevat*. The Mishna called it the "New Year of the Trees." In Palestine the day marks the beginning of the season of the budding of the trees and the planting of fruit trees. The Jews in the Diaspora designated the day for enjoying fruits native to Palestine, usually the carob (St. Jacob's bread) which, as the cheapest, is accessible even to the poor. The festival character of this day is marked in the orthodox ritual by the omitting of the supplicational prayers in the morning and in the afternoon service. The newly established colonies in Palestine made the day an "arbor day." In 1913 there was introduced into the Jewish public schools in Palestine the custom that the children march out into the fields to plant trees and to celebrate the "New Year" by eating fruit and singing special songs. The celebration of the day has been carried into many Jewish schools in other countries, used as means by which to strengthen the sentiments for Palestine in the heart of the youth.

# *P*URIM

## *(The Feast of Lots)*

*T*HE Thirteenth of Adar (in a leap year, Second *Adar—
Adar Sheni*) is the Fast of Esther—*Taanith Esther*. The
evening of that day and the whole of the day following,
constitute *Purim*—the Feast of Lots. Both days commemo-
rate the Jews' escape from impending doom, as related in
the Biblical book of Esther.

Unbeknown to her royal husband Ahasuerus, Esther—
Queen of Persia—was a Jewess. Her cousin, Mordecai, by reason of his loyalty to
his faith, had incurred
the ill-will of a certain
Haman, then in high
favor at court. With a
vengeance so often re-
peated in Jewish his-
tory, Haman retaliated
against the one hated
Jew, by scheming the
extermination of Mor-
decai's whole people,
the Jews. He pur-
chased a royal decree
for their wholesale
slaughter, justifying
his act by the in-

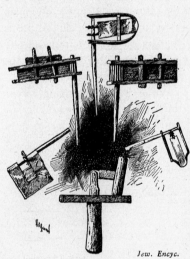

*Jew. Encyc.*

HAMAN-DREHERS

34

dictment that "their laws are different from those of every people; neither keep they the king's laws." Discovering the plot for the apparently inescapable massacre of the Jews, Mordecai importunes Esther to risk her life, disclose her identity to the king, and plead for her people's deliverance. After a day of fasting (hence the Fast of Esther), the queen approaches Ahasuerus. The treachery of Haman is disclosed, past unrequited service of Mordecai is brought to light; and with oriental pageantry the righteous are saved.

*Purim*—is considered a *Galuth* (Exile) Feast, that is a celebration in which the episodes just related stand as symbol of all the struggles of the Jewish people among the nations; of all the accusations, misrepresentations, tribulations, and dangers, suffered because we are repeatedly decried as "different from every people." While *Purim* is called a half-holiday, the Talmud declares that, though traditional festivals be neglected, *Purim* will never vanish—meaning that events celebrated by other special days may lose their reality, but that the sad events that created a *Purim* recur ever and again, and are poignantly meaningful.

*Purim* was observed already several centuries before the destruction of the Second Temple. It is mentioned in II Maccabees, 15:43.

On the evening of the thirteenth of *Adar*, the *Megillah*—the parchment scroll

Illuminated Megillah in Silver Case Illustrating the Story of Esther.
(H. U. C. Collection)

ILLUMINATED MEGILLAH (H. U. C. Library)

containing the book of Esther—is read in the synagogue. The traditional chant employed for it, is colorful and unique. The reading is interrupted at every mention of the name of Haman by the raucous whirring and buzzing of the *Haman-dreher* or *Klapper*, in the hands of the young people. After the reading, the Hebrew song *Shoshanath Yaakov* is

36

chanted. In the morning after the service the reading of the *Megillah* is repeated.

The home table differentiates the day by serving *Kreplach* and the special triangular poppy-seed cakes called *Homontashen* (literally: Haman-pockets). The German name for poppy-seed, *Mohn,* was associated with *Homon* or *Haman.*

The day was always dedicated to the remembering of the poor, and to the sending of gifts: *Shalach manoth* to friends. Since Talmudic times, *Purim* has been a day of gaiety, the one day in the year, on which the Jew permitted himself to indulge in banqueting and joy. He would burn Haman in effigy, remembering so many contemporary Hamans. From early performances of comedies based upon the story of Esther, the *"Purim* Plays" gradually developed.

Often fine artistry was displayed in the *Megillah*—drawings and paintings of scenes of the book of Esther, in its margins; carving in silver and wood for its case.

*Purim* in this country, has been a day for rehearsing its dramatic tale among the children, and for masque-dances among young and old. There is a noticeable increase in its use again as a day of gift giving. We should not let the distinctive chant of the *Megillah* be lost to us!

The day following is called *Shushan-Purim,* because (according to Esther 9:18-19) in Susa, the Persian capital, Purim was celebrated a day later. In commemoration of that belated observance, Purim is kept on the 15th of Adar in cities which are surrounded with a wall. In Jerusalem this custom is observed to the present time.

# *P*ESACH
### *(Passover)*

*P*ESACH is one of the most significant Jewish festivals. It commemorates Israel's liberation from Egyptian bondage and his becoming a free people awakened to the determination to serve none but the One God. The festival is, therefore, called *Zeman cheruthenu*—the season of our Liberty.

*Pesach* starts on the evening of the fourteenth of *Nissan,* and lasts for seven days. On account of the uncertainty of the old Jewish calendar, an eighth day was added, which was retained even after the calendar was stabilized (see Calendar). This additional eighth day has been abolished by the Reform group in America.

The name *Pesach* means "pass over"; and refers to the account in Exodus 12, that when the angel of death killed the first born of the Egyptians, he "passed over" the houses of the Israelites, which had all been carefully marked with a sprinkling of lamb-blood on the doorposts. In commemoration of this "passing over" every householder of ancient Israel was required to slaughter a lamb on the evening of the fourteenth of *Nissan,* pour its blood upon the altar of the Temple and roast its meat for his family's food. Another name of the festival: *Chag hammatzoth*—the Feast of Unleavened Bread—grows out of the Biblical narrative of the manner in which the Israelites—driven in haste out of Egypt—carried with them, dough still unleavened. As a yearly remembrance of this emergency, the people were commanded to eat only unleavened bread for one entire week. In order that destitute Jews be enabled to fulfill this command, funds, *Maoth chittim,* have always been collected before *Pesach* for the purchase of *matzoth* and wine for all not able to provide for themselves.

PASSOVER PLATE

*Courtesy, A. M. Burd, Germantown, Pa.*
*Designed and made by Reuben Leaf, New York City.*

Both the slaughtering of the lamb and the eating of un-leavened bread are customs originating before and inde-pendently of Israel. Arabic Bedouins to the present day, eat unleavened bread; while in the Near East, the slaughtering of lambs is an important feature of practically every religious and secular festivity. The *date of Pesach,* too, was long

39

observed among Semitic tribes, as a season of festivity. But out of these dissociated customs, Israel molded a unified holiday; and into them Israel infused the great idea of national and personal liberty, employing the concept of the "Season of Spring" figuratively as a "Season of Freedom."

With the destruction of the Temple, the Spring-assemblages of the people at the Sanctuary were terminated; and like all other sacrifices, the sacrifice of the Paschal lamb was abolished. The sages of that time, seeking to create substitute means of impressing and strengthening Israel's hope for and his high ideal of freedom, composed the *"Haggadah"* a ritual built on the "Tale of Passover," to be observed in the home—the Jew's Sanctuary.

Preparatory to *Pesach,* comes house-cleaning, the ritual requirement of which is the ridding of the place of all leaven (*Chametz*) and the removing or cleaning of vessels used for *Chametz*. The ceremonial search for remnants of leaven (*Bedikath chametz*) is observed in Orthodox homes on the evening of the thirteenth of *Nissan*. Whatever is discovered is burned the following morning. After the noon hour of the fourteenth of *Nissan,* no pious Jew would eat either *Chametz* or *Matzah*. On the evening of the fourteenth, *Pesach* is initiated by a service in the synagogue, followed by the home *Seder* (literally: Order), a special meal with accompanying ritual commemorative of the Exodus from Egypt. In Orthodox circles, *Seder* is still observed on the first two evenings, the duplication arising originally from the instability of the ancient calendar.

For the *Seder* the dining room is illumined with the festival lamps or candles; the table is decked in the household's best linens and silver. At the left of each seat is placed a cushion—originally a luxury of oriental noblemen, here, symbolic of the Jew's freedom. The table is laden with symbols: Three cakes of *Matzah* are covered with a special cloth on which are embroidered or printed the benedictions over the *Matzah*. *Pesach*-wine of grapes or raisins, is served at each place in a tumbler of silver or glass (Hebrew—*Kos*) on which there are frequently engraved or painted the benediction over wine and various Jewish symbols. A large silver dish (Hebrew—*Kaarah*) holds a roasted lamb bone, commemorative of the Paschal lamb; a roasted egg, a substitute for the ancient holiday sacrifice (*Korban chagigah*); a root of horseradish (*Maror —bitter herb*) symbol of the bitterness endured in Egypt; a sprig of parsley or watercress (*Karpas*); and *Charoseth,* a compound of ground apples, raisins and almonds mixed with cinnamon and wine, which by its appearance serves as a reminder of the clay from which our ancestors were forced to make bricks for Pharaoh. There is a special cup filled with wine, called *Kos shel Eliyahu*—the cup of the Prophet Elijah, who according to Jewish legend, visits every *Seder,* and who—at the end of days—will bring the tidings of the Messianic age. Each person present is pro-

THE CUP OF ELIJAH

*Courtesy, A. M. Burd, Germantown, Pa. Designed and made by Reuben Leaf, New York City.*

41

vided with a *Haggadah.* Before beginning the ritual, the
father used to put on his *Kittl* (white shroud).

The table service opens with the chanting of the *Kiddush,*
followed by the drinking of the first cup (*Kos*) of wine.
*Karpas* is served. Originally this was an appetizer. The
master of the house breaks the middle of the three *Matzoth,*
part of which (called *Aphikomon*—Greek for "dessert") he
hides to be discovered and eaten at the conclusion of the
meal. As he lifts the *Matzah* he recites: "This is the bread
of affliction," etc. The youngest person present, usually a
child, asks the "Four Questions": (1) Why on this night,
do we eat only unleavened bread? (2) Why do we eat
*Maror?* (3) Why do we eat *Charoseth?* and (4) Why do
we observe the ceremony of *Seder?* The leader answers
these questions by relating the story of Israel in Egypt and
of the Exodus conducted by Moses that he might bring
Israel to the acceptance of the teachings of the One God.
The *Hallel* (Psalms 113-114) is then sung, and the second
cup of wine taken. *Matzah-Maror,* and *Charoseth* are dis-
tributed to all.

The service is here interrupted by the meal at which it is
customary to serve hard boiled eggs dipped in salt water,
and *matzah*-balls (*Kneidlach,* from German *Knoedel*). At
the end of the meal, there is a scramble among the children
to discover the hidden *Matzah,* necessary for the conclusion
of the dinner. The fortunate one receives a prize. Dinner
over, grace is chanted; and the third cup of wine drunk.
The assemblage then chants the second part of *Hallel*
(Psalms 115-118), takes the fourth cup of wine; and sings
several old Hebrew folksongs, such as *Addir hu* (God of
Might), *Ki lo noe* (Our souls we raise); and two especially
devised to interest the children: *Echad mi yode'a* (Who

knows one?) and *Chad gadya* (An only Kid.)  All of these have been translated into both German and English. Their tunes were composed by Jewish singers during the last three centuries. According to old custom, before the conclusion of the *Seder,* the door is opened for the Prophet Elijah.

FRONTISPIECE
OF THE
UNION
HAGGADAH

Published by
The Central Conference
of American Rabbis.

Few books of the Jewish library have been more carefully and frequently edited and published than the ritual of the *Seder,* the *Haggadah*. During the Middle Ages, the art of illuminating and illustrating it was highly developed, producing art letters, ornamented title pages, marginal paintings and drawings of the Exodus story, symbolic figures portray-

43

ing the religious and ethical interpretations, as derived from the text by the rabbis.

Many wonderful manuscripts have been preserved, some of which have recently been published. Of these, the Sarayevo, Darmstadt, and Frankfort *Haggadahs* rank first. Among modern *Haggadahs,* we note especially the "Revised Union Haggadah" published by the Central Conference of American Rabbis. In its art of ornamentation, in its presentation of the text, and last but not least in its addition of traditional *Seder* music, it is the highest achievement in *Haggadah* making, and the most suitable *Haggadah* for use by the modern Jew.

The *Seder* has survived in the Jewish home through every exigency of history. Practiced in secret by the Maranos in the days of the Inquisition, celebrated in the teeth of the relentless mobs with the threats of the old "blood accusation," the *Seder* persists as an emblem and promise of freedom. It ever was and still is the high spot of religious home ceremonies.

# Sefirah
## Lag Baomer

ON the second evening of Passover, "counting" (*Sefirah*) starts, and continues for forty-nine days until *Shabuoth*. This reckoning commemorates the ancient daily sacrifice, on the Temple altar, of a sheaf (*Omer*) of the first ripened ears, as commanded in Leviticus 23:10, 11. In the Orthodox Synagogue, after each evening service, announcement is made of the number of days that has passed. A special benediction is followed by a silent prayer. During the *Sefirah*-season certain signs of mourning are observed in Orthodox

*Jew. Encyc.*

TRADITIONAL GRAVE OF RABBI SIMEON BAR YOCHAI
AT TIME OF PILGRIMAGE

45

circles, such as refraining from having one's hair cut, permitting no weddings or other festivities. The mourning was ordered by the sages to remind us of the unsuccessful uprising of Bar Kochba (about 125 C. E.) against the crushing Roman yoke, and the terrible massacre of over half a million Jews that followed the quelling of that revolt. It is recorded that twenty-four thousand of Rabbi Akiba's disciples were killed during the fight.

Because the massacre stopped on the thirty-third day of *Sefirah* (*Lag Baomer*) this day was designated as a day on which God showed mercy to the remnant of Israel. Therefore on this day, children are given boiled eggs—a dish served to mourners; and celebrations are permitted.

During the Middle Ages, the cabalists in Palestine instituted a celebration on *Lag Baomer,* in memory of the legendary Rabbi Simeon Bar Yochai, because on this day, he was supposed to have revealed his cabalistic secrets to his disciples. The annual celebration is held in Meron, a village near Safed, Palestine, to which place thousands of people pilgrim.

# Shabuoth
## (*The Feast of Weeks*)

S HABUOTH occurs six weeks after *Pesach,* on the evening of the fifth of *Siwan.* Originally only one day was celebrated; but later, on account of the unsettled calendar, a second was added. As with other holidays, so in the case of

Jew. Encyc.

TABLES OF THE LAW FROM AN ITALIAN SYNAGOGUE
—Dated 1671

this one, Reform Judaism reinstituted the original one day. *Shabuoth* is recorded in the Bible as *Chag Habbikkurim—*

the feast of the offering of the first of the ripe crop. It was an agricultural festival observed in Palestine in ancient times. On account of its being the fiftieth day of *Sefirah,* this feast was called *Pentecost,* by the Greek speaking Jews.

Quite independently of this nature feast, Exodus 19 describes the great event of the giving of the Ten Commandments on Mt. Sinai, as occurring on the third day of *Siwan.* Thus *Shabuoth* came to be celebrated also as the festival of the giving of the *Torah* to Israel (*Zeman Mattan Torathenu*). After the destruction of the Temple, it was this latter idea which gave content to *Shabuoth.* Throughout the entire night preceding *Shabuoth* it became customary to read the *Tikkun*—excerpts from the first and last chapters of all Biblical books, as well as from the *Mishnah.* The synagogue used to be decorated with green branches and flowers, in commemoration of the original harvest-character of the festival. The service of the day includes the reading of the Ten Commandments. Also the book of Ruth is read because of its heroine's acceptance of Israel's religion. Many Hebrew hymns have been created for this service.

At home, dairy foods and honey are served, symbolizing Israel's joy in the *Torah,* which is compared to "milk and honey," that is nourishing and sweet.

The Synagogue is decorated with greenery as a symbol of the perennial freshness of the *Torah.*

The first leaders of the Reform Movement selected, for the "Confirmation" of Jewish boys and girls, this day of *Shabuoth* on which—according to tradition—Israel was first confirmed in its faith, by Moses. The custom has proved successful in its impressiveness upon the youth and in its revitalization of the festival.

# TISH'A BE'AB
# THE THREE WEEKS

SOME of the Jewish festivals have had historical significance read into them. Others, however, such as *Chanukah,* were instituted in commemoration of actual events. Of
the latter kind is also the season of the three weeks of mourning over the destruction of the two successive Temples in Jerusalem, over the devastation of the Jewish homeland in Palestine, and over the subsequent dispersion of the people to all
the corners of the globe. This period starts with the fast of the
seventeenth of *Tammuz* and concludes with the fast of the
Ninth of *Ab* (*Tish'a Be'ab*), the day on which the Temples
were burned. No festivity, no putting on of new clothes, no
dedication of new buildings, is permissible during these three
weeks. On the last nine days, pious people refrain from eat-

TISH'A
BE'AB

*L. Horowitz*

49

ing meat—symbol of the sacrifices offered in the Temple.

On the day of the concluding twenty-four hour fast, wor-shippers in the synagogue remove their shoes and sit upon the floor as a sign of mourning. The men use neither the *Tallith* nor the *Tefillin* in the morning service. The book of Lamentations is chanted in a traditional mournful tune, and many prayers and poems of lamentative character are recited. In the evening, the synagogue is but dimly illuminated. From the Ark, the curtains are removed, symbolizing that the *Torah* too, is in mourning.

For almost nineteen hundred years the whole Jewish peo-ple bewailed its loss of a national and spiritual centre, and ex-pressed its deep sorrow over this calamity, by fasting and by praying and hoping for the rebuilding of the Temple in Jeru-salem. Reform Judaism, while viewing the day as one com-memorating historic tragedy, does not observe it with fasting.

*E. Bendemann*

JEREMIAH AT THE FALL OF JERUSALEM

# THE JEWISH CALENDAR

SINCE all of our Jewish festivals are set according to the Jewish Calendar, it is important that we familiarize ourselves with its system.

The Jewish calendar is based on *lunar* reckonings. The circling of the moon around the earth constitutes a month. The day following the evening on which the new moon is first perceived is called *Rosh Chodesh*—New Moon. In ancient Israel this day was considered as important a festival as Sabbath. In the course of time this day lost much of its significance. It is at present observed in Orthodox circles, by special insertions in the services, such as *Yaale Veyavo* and *Musaf*, by the chanting of the *Hallel* and by the reading of a portion of the Pentateuch (Numbers 28:11-15), dealing with the sacrifices for this day. No mourning is permissible on *Rosh Chodesh*.

The day preceding each *Rosh Chodesh* is since the 17th century ordained a "Small Day of Atonement"—*Yom Kippur Katon*. On this day pious people fast and recite supplications.

Twelve lunar months constitute a year. The Jewish names of the months are: *Tishrè, Cheshwan, Kislew, Tebeth, Shebat, Adar, Nissan, Iyyar, Siwan, Tammuz, Ab, Elul.* The circling of the moon around the earth takes 29 days, 12 hours, 44 minutes and 3 seconds. In order to use round figures the five months *Tishrè, Shebat, Nissan, Siwan, Ab* were arranged with 30 and the five months *Tebeth, Adar, Iyyar, Tammuz* and *Elul* with 29 days. If the month has 29 days, one day *Rosh Chodesh* is observed, but if the month has 30 days two days *Rosh Chodesh* are celebrated, the last day of the outgoing and the first of the new month. The months *Cheswan* and *Kislev* have sometimes 29 and sometimes 30 days. The number is determined by the adjustment of the calendar, resulting from the fixing of the Day of Atonement (which, according to the Law, must never occur on a Friday or a Sunday) and of *Hoshana Rabba* (which must never fall on Saturday).

The twelve months total 354 days, 8 hours, 48 minutes and 36 seconds, against 365 days, 6 hours and 48 seconds of the solar year (according to the Jewish sages). Thus the lunar year is shorter than the solar year by about 10 days, 21 hours and 12 seconds. If we should reckon according to the lunar year only, it would come about that Passover and Succoth would fall sometimes in winter and sometimes in summer. We see this peculiar shifting of the festivals among the Mohammedans who too have the lunar calendar. The Bible distinctly orders that Passover be celebrated in the spring and Succoth be observed after the harvest in the fall season. Hence an adjustment was devised, between the lunar and solar years by the adding every two or three years, of the leap month *Adar Sheni*—the second *Adar*. These extra 29 days added to the regular 354 make the leap year 383 days; and provide for the accumulated shortage of approximately 11 days a year. From the explanations thus far given it is obvious, that the Jewish months can never run parallel with the months of the solar year. Therefore the Jewish Holidays fall, each year, on different dates of the civil calendar.

In olden times in Palestine the beginning of the month was determined in a primitive way. On the day when the new moon was expected people were sent, at sunset, to the shore of the Mediterranean, where the horizon is unobstructed, to watch for the appearance of the new moon. As soon as two people reported having seen it, the Jewish supreme court announced the beginning of the month. This news was then immediately relayed by the fire-signals hoisted by special watchmen on the peaks of the mountains, so that during the night the word spread all over the country. Later however, the hostile Samaritans, in order to deceive the people, would send out false fire-signals. Therefore the Jews abandoned this method, and instead, sent trustworthy messengers to carry tidings of the new moon. This means of course, was slow. At times, the messengers could not reach all the communities, especially those beyond the limits of Palestine. These would be left in doubt as to the exact day of the new moon and holiday celebrations were correspondingly delayed. Therefore the High Court in Jerusalem issued the order that the Jews outside of Palestine should celebrate each of the principal festivals two days. This usage persisted even after the permanent calendar was established and sanctioned by Hillel II, Jewish Prince in Palestine in 360 C. E., and the custom survives to this day. Reform Judaism, however, abolished it.

In Palestine, all holidays—with the exception of *Rosh-Hashanah*—have always been celebrated but one day. Originally this holiday too lasted only one day. But it once happened that through error, the new moon was announced one day ahead of time. The spiritual leaders, in their anxiety to have the new year begin as exactly as possible, ordered, shortly before the destruction of the Second Temple, that thereafter *Rosh Hashanah* be celebrated two days: the first and the second day of *Tishrè*. In this case too, Reform Judaism returned to the original one day.

## II

# DAILY CEREMONIES IN HOME AND SYNAGOGUE

*"I set the Lord before me at all times."
This statement of the Psalmist (16:8)
voices the thought underlying the various religious customs in the daily
life of the Jew.*

# $T$ZITZITH

$T$ZITZITH (fringe) means white threads with which a cord of sky-blue is entwined, originally fastened to the four corners of the robe, which men in the Orient customarily wore. This robe, called *Tallith,* was a square piece of woolen cloth (somewhat similar to the *abaye* of the Arabs) in which the people used to wrap themselves. According to Numbers 15:38-40, the custom of attaching the fringe to each corner, was commanded "that you may look upon it and remember all the commandments of the Lord and do them; and that ye go not about after your own heart and your own eyes after which ye use to go astray." The *Tzi-*

*S. Bender*

WINDING THE TZITZITH ON THE TALLITH

57

TALLITH (Showing Tzitzith in Corners)

*tzith* served as the Jew's uniform, whereby he was recognized and distinguished from the gentile. The blue cord entwined in the fringe was its principal distinction. The use of blue is thus explained in the Talmud: "Because this color resembles the sea; the sea resembles the sky; and the sky resembles the 'chair of Glory'." The method of dying the threads sky-blue, was a secret of the people in Acre, Palestine. After the dispersion, the art was forgotten by the Jews in the Diaspora, and the use of the blue thread was discontinued.

Four white threads are drawn through each of the four corners of the *Tallith* or *Tallith Katan,* and a double knot is made with one of the threads which is longer than the others and is called *"Shamash."* The other threads are wound according to the following order: 7 windings and a double knot, 8 windings and a double knot, 11 windings and a double knot and 13 windings and a double knot. If 2 of the 8 threads are torn off, the *Tzitzith* is not considered valid. The 39 windings represent the numerical value of יהוה אחד.

In the course of time, the Jews, adopting the costumes of the lands of their residence, could no longer attach *Tzitzith* to their main garment. The *Tallith* was retained but its use restricted to the Synagogue during the morning service. Its fringes are kissed, and a benediction is pronounced, as it is wrapped about the worshipper. In order to fulfill the Biblical injunction to wear "fringes" at all times, a substitute was devised in the *Tallith Katan* (small *Tallith*), otherwise called *Arba-Kanfoth* (four corners). This is a rectangular piece of linen, silk, or woolen cloth, with *Tzitzith* on its four corners, and an opening in the center large enough to admit the head. Resting on the shoulders, it hangs over the chest and back; and is worn under the garments. The use of the large *Tallith* was obligatory for only the adult males —according to the custom of some countries, beginning with the youth's marriage; according to that of other lands, dating from his *Bar Mitzvah* ceremony (at the age of thirteen). The duty of wearing the small *Tallith,* on the other hand, rests upon every male, from early boyhood. No pious Jew would walk even "four steps" without it. Reform Judaism in America employs neither the *Arba Kanfoth* nor the *Tallith.*

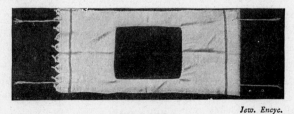

ARBA KANFOTH

*Jew. Encyc.*

# TEFILLIN
## *(Phylacteries or Frontlets)*

AS soon as a Jew rises in the morning, his first duty is to prepare himself for the morning service—*Teffilath Shacharith*. After washing his hands and face, he recites: "I thank thee, O King, living and eternal God, that thou hast in mercy returned to me my soul. Great is Thy faithfulness."

The use of the *Tefillin* is based on an interpretation of the statements in Exodus 13:9 and Deut. 6:8. In ancient times, protecting amulets were worn on head and hands. With the development of loftier ideas in Judaism, this custom was re-interpreted to remind the wearer of his duties to God. "As long as the *Tefillin* are on the head and the arm of a man," say the sages, "he is modest and God-fearing, will not be attracted by hilarity or idle talk, and will have no evil thoughts; but will devote his mind wholly to truth and righteousness."

The name *Tefillin* (singular *Tefilla*) is derived from *Tefilla* (prayer). The objects consist of two square black leather boxes (*Batim*), one worn on the left arm (called *Shel Yad*), and the other (*Shel Rosh*) worn on the forehead where the hairgrowth starts. The boxes are made of the skins of Levitically "clean" animals. They are backed with square pieces of thick leather, and sealed by means of twelve stitches made with threads prepared from the veins of "clean" animals. At their corners are strap-loops through which are passed leather straps cut from the skin of "clean" animals and blackened on the top. The strap that runs through the loops of the head-phylactery is fastened in a circle large enough to fit onto the head, by means of a knot in the shape of the Hebrew letter ד. The one that passes through the loops of the hand phylactery, forms a noose near the box, that is fastened by a knot in the shape of the letter י. The head-box has on the outside, the letter ש to the

PRAYING JEW
WITH TALLITH
AND TEFILLIN

M. P. *Klodt*

right while to the left the same letter has four strokes. These three letters are those of the Hebrew word שדי —*Shadday* (Almighty). The head-box contains four compartments which hold as many bits of parchment, each inscribed with one of the four Biblical passages: Exodus 13:1-10, Exodus 13:11-16; Deuteronomy 6:4-9; and Deuteronomy 11:13-21. The head-box has only one compartment to hold one parchment sheet on which all the four passages are written.

Every man from the age of thirteen, is obliged to use the *Tefillin* for each week-day morning service, whether he worships in the Synagogue or at home. The Jew does not employ them on Sabbaths and holidays, because these days—being

S. *Bender*

TEACHING A BOY TO PUT ON TEFILLIN

in themselves religious symbols—are accounted sufficient reminders of his religious duties.

As the *Tefillin* are drawn from their containers they are kissed. The hand-phylactery is put on first. Its box is set on the inside of the left arm (the arm nearer to the heart), just above the elbow. Its strap is wound seven times around the arm, and three additional times around the hand in the form of the letter ש. Then the strap circle of the head-phylactery is set onto the head, bringing the box over the center of the forehead, and the strap-knot low on the head at the center-back, the ends of the straps being thrown front over the shoulders. While adjusting the *Tefillin,* the man recites a benediction, and when the arrangement is completed, he quotes Hosea 2:21-22.

Many great rabbis used to wear *Tefillin* all the day long. Only people in clean places, able to devote themselves entirely to meditations and the study of the holy teachings are permitted to wear *Tefillin* the whole day.

Women, exempted by law from the duty of *Tefillin* and *Tallith* used to manifest their religious devotion by embroidering bags for the *Tefillin* and the *Tallith* of their husbands, sons or brothers.

DAVEN = PRAYER, DEVOTIONS

# Mezuzah

THE name *Mezuzah* is the Hebrew word for door-post, to which place this ceremonial object is fastened. The *Mezuzah* is a small wooden, glass, or metal case or tube, containing a rolled rectangular piece of parchment inscribed with the passages: Deuteronomy 6:4-9 and 11:13-21. On the outer side of the parchment, near the top of the roll, is written the word *Shadday;* and an opening is left in the case opposite the word. The *Mezuzah* is affixed in a slanting position, to

THE
MEZUZAH

the upper part of the door-post at one's right as he enters the dwelling, the upper end of the box pointing inward and the lower one outward. Pious Jews kiss their fingers after they touch the *Mezuzah,* reciting: "May God keep my going out and my coming in, from now on and evermore." The fastening of it to the door-post is accompanied by a benediction. Among modern Jews, the *Mezuzah* has fallen into disuse.

Just as *Tzitzith* and *Tefillin* originated as charms to protect the body from evil spirits, so also to the *Mezuzah* was ascribed the power of warding off from the house all harm from without. And just as into the former two objects a higher religious conception was later read, so also new meaning was given the *Mezuzah.* The Biblical command reads: "And Thou shalt write them (the laws of God) upon the door-posts of thy house, and upon thy gates." (Deuteronomy 6:9). Maimonides thus explains the value of the *Mezuzah.* "By the commandment of the *Mezuzah,* man is reminded, when coming or going, of the unity of God, and is aroused to the love of Him. He is awakened from his slumber and has vain worldly thoughts to the realization that nothing endures in eternity as the knowledge of the Rock of the World. This contemplation brings him back to himself and leads him on the right path."

The Talmud says: "Whoever has *Tefillin* on his head and arm, *Tzitzith* on his garments, and a *Mezuzah* on his door, gives assurance that he will not commit sins."

# *T*ABLE *C*EREMONIES

**B**EFORE all meals at which bread is served (it being considered the main part of a meal) the Jew is obliged to wash his hands and while doing so, to pronounce a benediction, because he is to be purified for the table as a priest for the altar on which sacrifices are made. Therefore a certain sanctity attached to the meal. A benediction must be recited over bread, which is frequently dipped in salt as a remembrance of the way the sacrifices used to be salted. "If three have eaten at a table and have spoken there no words of Torah, it is as if they had eaten of sacrifices to dead idols" (Ethics of the Fathers 3:4). After the meal, on week-days, Psalm 137 and grace are chanted.

FLEISHIG = meat ⎫ don't mix.
MILCHIG = milk ⎭

# $\mathcal{T}$HE $\mathcal{D}$IETARY $\mathcal{L}$AWS

ALREADY in ancient Israel there existed customs pertaining to food. Only vegetables were permitted without restrictions, whereas for certain fruit, such as grapes, laws defined when and how their use was permitted. Similarly grain was subjected to rules such as sacrificing on the altar the first ripe sheaves and giving to the priests a certain quantity before the rest might be used. Laws prohibited even the planting together of grain and fruit. However, most restrictions were laid upon the use of meat. In the first place only a limited number of kinds of animals, fowl, and fish, was permitted. In Leviticus XI rules are given according to which the permitted, the *clean* (*Kosher*) ones, should be recognized, and the names are listed of the *unclean* kinds which should not be tasted, the milk and eggs of which should not be eaten, and the dead bodies of which should not be touched. But even the use of the permitted kinds was manifoldly restricted.

In ancient Israel, if one wanted to eat meat, he had to bring the animal or the bird, usually a pigeon, as a sacrifice to the altar. The priest slaughtered it, dashed the blood against the altar, and burned parts of the fat upon the altar. Certain parts of the sacrificed animal belonged to the priest. At a later time it became permissible to slaughter animals without sacrificing (Deut. 12:21); but the eating of the blood was emphatically prohibited, "for the blood is the life" (Deut. 12:23). This regulation was enforced by the sages to such an extent that even a drop of blood found in the yolk, makes the egg forbidden food, because it is accounted evidence that the process of hatching has already begun. The customs of ritual slaughtering, of refraining from the eating of blood, of certain fat, and of the *unclean* kinds of living creatures, have been retained.

The method of prescribed slaughtering (in Hebrew *Shechita*) is the cutting through of the wind pipe and the gullet in mammals, or either of these in birds, with a specially prepared knife (in Hebrew *Chalaf*). This knife must be sharp and smooth, without notches, so that the cut shall not be interrupted, and shall not cause unnecessary pain to the animal. The knife must be without a point, must be of pure steel, and its length must be at least twice the width of the neck of the animal. There are three sizes: a small one for fowl, a larger one for small cattle, and the largest size for big animals. For such killing, an expert slaughterer (*Shochet*) is required, who, having studied the code of laws pertaining to ritual slaughtering, has been examined, and provided with a certificate (*Kabbalah*) by a rabbi, and has practiced under the guidance of an experienced *Shochet*. Before slaughtering, the *Shochet* has to examine the smoothness of the edge of the knife with the nail of his forefinger, then he must examine the fowl or animal, to make sure that there is not a defective limb, or some other deficiency which, according to the Law, would make it unfit to eat. Then he has to pronounce a certain Hebrew benediction. It is an old custom that the blood of a fowl be covered with ashes. After the slaughtering is performed, the knife has to be examined to ascertain whether a notch was made in it during the process of cutting. In such case the object slaughtered is declared unfit (*Trefah*). This is also the case if at least the

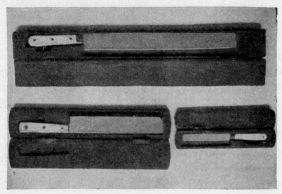

Jew. Encyc.

SLAUGHTERING KNIVES

greater part of the two before-mentioned organs in mammals or of one in fowl, are not cut through. In addition, in mammals, the lungs have to be examined by the *Shochet* to determine whether they are affected with tuberculosis or with some other disease recorded in the code. In case of slight touches of tuberculosis in the lungs, the soundness of the liver determines the ritual cleanness (*Kashruth*) of the animal. Every stomach must be examined. In prescribing these tests, the sages declared that "a diseased animal cannot live," that is that the disease must finally overcome the animal's vitality, and that for the sake of the health of the person, meat of such an animal must not be eaten.

The prohibition of blood was extended even to the blood that comes forth from the meat. Therefore, the Jew was commanded to keep meat in water for half an hour and then in salt for an hour, so that the blood be extracted. There was further required the extraction of certain veins of blood and vessels of fat running through the body of the animal. (This

69

procedure is called *treibern* in Yiddish, *Nikkur* in Hebrew.)
Fish and locusts—the latter eaten in the Orient—are not
subjected to ritual slaughtering.

Interdiction was pronounced on the eating of milk, butter,
cheese, or any other dairy dish, with meat or with any food
prepared with meat. In their stern strict manner the rabbis
ordered special sets of dishes for meat and for dairy food.
The Bible prohibition reads only: "Thou shalt not seethe a
kid in its mother's milk" (Ex. 23:19; 34:26; Deut. 14:21).
Judging from the severity that the law acquired and the
strictness of its observance during so many centuries, we may
presume that this custom of separating meat from milk dates
back originally to a very early time. Honey was adjudged
a permitted food since it is merely the juice of the flower
gathered by the bee and then secreted; and contains no portion of the bee which, as an insect, is prohibited.

The idea underlying all these restrictions is given in
Leviticus 11:44: "Sanctify yourselves therefore, and be ye
holy; for I am holy; neither shall ye defile yourselves with
any manner of swarming thing that moveth upon the earth."
And Deut. 14:3 admonishes: "Thou shalt not eat any abom-
inable thing." Some sages regard the dietary laws as restrictions that grew out of old taboos. Some think that ritual
slaughtering was ordered to prevent cruelty, because in olden
times Israel's neighbors used to cut off limbs of living animals and eat them (Deut. 12:23). Again others maintain the
idea that all dietary laws, those pertaining to slaughtering
as well as the rules about *clean* and *unclean* animals, grew
out of hygienic precautions. They are convinced that people who eat *unclean* animals incur diseases and further bring
a bad effect upon their spirit. Many modern scientists too are
convinced that the method of ritual slaughtering is the best

and least painful of all methods. Indeed the dietary laws exerted a great influence upon the Jewish people through the dark centuries—living as they did, amidst people of a much lower cultural level, people with no hygienic principles and no boards of health. These laws saved the Jews from many diseases transmitted through unhealthy food of infected animals. They also exerted a strong psychological influence, in that the Jew believed that the conscientious observance of the dietary laws helped to keep him clean in body and in spirit.

# THE COVERING OF THE HEAD

THE covering of the head was always customary in Israel at religious functions. The priests had to wear mitres or headdress while officiating (Exodus 28:36-38). At the beginning of the Common Era, the covering of the head began to be practiced not only for religious acts but at all times. Many sages did not walk "four steps" with uncovered head. This habit was considered symbolic of the fear of God. Especially during meals, to which a religious meaning was attached, nobody would uncover his head.

This custom is not a Jewish one exclusively. The Mohammedans too observe it religiously. It was accorded greater importance by Jews living among Christians who practiced the uncovering of the head as a sign of reverence. To make the observance easier, Orthodox Jews use a little cap, *Yarmulke* (a Slavic-Tartarian word) or (in German) *Kappel*. The emancipation of the Jews in the nineteenth century and their adoption of European customs brought about the neglect of the habit of covering their heads in daily life. Some of the Reform leaders advocated the uncovering of the head even at religious functions; and in 1845 the Reform Congregation in Berlin started worshipping bareheaded. The innovation, however, found no following in Europe. But in America it found adherents in the Reform group and was adopted in almost all Reform congregations. It became a stumbling block for many conservative minded Jews preventing them from joining the Reform movement. Thus we see that customs often loom larger than basic principles in religion. "Do not walk in the ways of the gentiles"—this precept was not so strictly observed in regard to many commandments as in the case of the custom of the covering of the head. Even Jews, who, in their daily life are negligent of the observance of many Biblical and Rabbinical precepts and do not practice the covering of the head, consider this custom most important in religious functions in the Synagogue. To worship bareheaded, they regard as a typical Christian form, for which Paul pleaded in saying: "Every man praying or prophesying, having his head covered dishonoureth his head" (1 Corinthians 11:4). The Reform attitude is that, inasmuch as the uncovering of the head became the manner of expressing reverence among all European and American people in their religious and secular life the Jew should not be singled out by different practice.

## THE SHEITEL

Married women used to cover their hair, as a sign of chastity. In the Orient a special hair-kerchief (*yazme*) is worn, while in Europe the *Sheitel* (German for wig) or *Perruk* (from French *perruque*) is customary. In ultra-orthodox circles women are obliged to cut short or even to shave off their hair on the eve of their wedding. Mohammedan women are urged to cover their faces completely at the approach of strange men. Among Jews as well as among Mohammedans this custom is gradually falling into disuse, with the progress of woman's emancipation.

# THE MIZRACH

THE Mizrach (literally: the Rising of the Sun; or the East) is a decorated motto or picture hung on the eastern wall in many Jewish homes and in front of the reading desk in the Synagogue. This sign gives the direction toward which Jews living west of Palestine turn while at prayer. The custom of turning in prayer, toward Jerusalem dates back to the time after the destruction of the first Temple. Jews who live east of Palestine turn toward the west, those who live south of it turn toward the north, and those who find themselves north of it turn toward the south. The Jews in Europe and America turn toward the east. In accordance with this

MIZRACH

74

custom, synagogues are so constructed that the ark may be placed on the eastern wall. Reform Judaism, emphasizing the conviction that God is everywhere, has built its synagogues facing no specific direction.

In the making of the *Mizrach*, considerable art has been expended. Usually Psalm 113:3 is inscribed in Hebrew. Some scenes of the Bible are drawn or the "Wailing Wall" in Jerusalem is sketched. An Orthodox Jew, who happens to be in a strange house, when the time of prayer comes, looks for the *Mizrach*, or else asks where the east is.

Thus the daily ceremonies effectively remind the Jew of his Judaism.

## III

# CEREMONIAL OBJECTS IN THE SYNAGOGUE

*Several objects in the Synagogue are institutions as old as is Judaism.*

# CEREMONIAL OBJECTS IN THE SYNAGOGUE

MANY objects in the Synagogue have been transmitted from the Temple in Jerusalem, and to the Temple from still older sanctuaries of Israel.

*Kiyor*. Near the entrance of the vestibule of the Orthodox Synagogue is the *Kiyor* (Laver), a water basin usually of engraved or wrought copper or brass. In the early Tabernacle and in the Jerusalem Temple the laver was designed for the ablution of the priests "when they come near to the altar to minister" (Ex. 30:20). Like many others, this priestly custom later became incumbent upon the whole of the priest-people; and every Jew was enjoined to wash his hands before praying. On Festivals, before the *Cohanim* (members of the priestly tribe) walk forward to bless the congregation, they wash their hands from this—or in some synagogues, a special laver, while the water is poured for them by *Levites* (members of the tribe of Levi). Hygienic and aesthetic considerations have ruled the *Kiyor* out of the modern Synagogue.

*Tzedakah Box*. Near the inner Synagogue door, are frequently fastened one or more boxes for various charities. According to the old Jewish attitude, prayer is acceptable only when combined with true repentance and with charity. And genuine charity is that given in secret. Even a person supported by charity is obliged to give, says the Talmud.

*Seating*. The Orthodox Synagogue is partitioned into the

chief division for men and a smaller secondary section for women. This latter is generally raised to a balcony along the western wall (that is the rear of the Synagogue auditorium). Sometimes it extends also along the northern and southern walls. This separation of the sexes during the service, is of ancient origin—instituted in Israel to preclude the ugly religious practices of the neighboring peoples, and to preserve purity of worship. The plans of the Temple in Jerusalem specify a woman's court (*Ezrath Nashim*). The arrangement continued unchallenged until the modern emancipation of woman.

Inasmuch as Reform flourishes only in those sections of the world where the modern standards of culture have placed men and women side by side in education, business, and social life, the Reform Synagogue has abolished the woman's gallery, and seated men and women together in worship. In some places, the family pew is customary.

Concerning the seating plan of the main Synagogue auditorium, there are two customs. In central and eastern Europe, in the Ashkenazic synagogues, the seats are arranged in rows facing the east, that is the front of the synagogue. The Reform Synagogue follows this plan (See *Mizrach*). In western Europe and in the near East, in Sephardic and Oriental synagogues, the seats are arranged in concentric rectangles, so as to face the *Almemor* or *Bema* (see Reading Desks below) which stands in the center. In many synagogues in central and western Europe special seats are built either in front of the *Almemor* or *Bema* or against the northern wall, for the president, vice-president and secretary of the congregation. This custom is not known in Eastern Europe. From Talmudic times, seats along the *Mizrach* (eastern) wall have been a sign of special honor. In the

Reform Synagogue special chairs for the president and vice-president are, like those for the rabbi and cantor, set on the platform.

*Reading Desks.* The *Almemor* (Arabic: *Al-mimbar,* orator pulpit) or *Bema* (Greek for speaker's tribune) is an elevated platform with a reading desk, originally placed in center of the Synagogue. It was instituted in emulation of Ezra's raised pulpit, and for the same purpose, that is the reading of the Book of the Law (Nehemiah 8:4-8). Such a platform and desk were built in the court of the Second Temple; and thence transplanted into the Synagogue. In the course of time there developed two manners of using it. The Ashkenazim employ the *Bema,* as originally intended, for reading the Torah and for making announcements, whereas the Sephardim use it also as the desk from which the precentor recites the prayers. Some Ashkenazic synagogues in English countries adopted this Sephardic custom. Certain Portuguese synagogues have drawn the *Almemor* back to the western wall.

The *Amud* or Prayer-desk since Talmudic days, has been set before the Ark, or at times to the right of it. The reader or *chazzan* stands at the *Amud* with his back to the congregation, facing the Ark, to pronounce the prayers. The Talmud emphasizes that the floor of the Prayer-desk should be lower than that of the Synagogue, that the reader may speak as did the Psalmist: "Out of the depths have I called Thee, O Lord" (130:1). In front of the desk there is usually a *Mizrach* (see this) with some Biblical phrases inscribed, such as "Know before whom thou standest," or "I behold my Lord before me always." The *Amud,* as already insinuated, is used in the Ashkenazic synagogues only.

In the modernized Orthodox synagogues, the *Bema* has

POLISH SYNAGOGUE AT VIENNA

*Jew. Encyc.*

been drawn up to the *Amud* and either the two desks become one, or the *Amud* stands close to the Ark and the *Bema* a little further from it.

The Reform Synagogue has but one desk, set on a platform at the front. From it the prayers and Torah are read and the sermon delivered. The reader at all times faces the congregation.

The *Aron-hakodesh* (the Ark of the Holiness) is placed at the eastern wall either as a niche built into the wall or as a chest fastened onto or protruding from it. It has always been customary for the Synagogue to be so constructed that the worshippers, when turning toward the Ark, face in the direction of Jerusalem. For the Jews of Europe and America, this has meant that the front wall of the synagogue auditorium be on the east. The ark is set on an elevated platform against the eastern wall, and is approached by steps. It is a reminder of the Biblical Ark of the Covenant in which the Tables of the Law were placed. In the *Aron hakodesh,* the Torah (Five Books of Moses) is kept. As a rule the Ark contains more than one scroll. Large and old synagogues own thirty to fifty scrolls, donated by members of the congregation. The presentation of a scroll to the synagogue has ever been considered a great merit. The Ark is lined with silk or velvet. In it are specially formed stands to support the scrolls. The designing and ornamenting of the Ark have afforded expression for some exquisite art. Despite the prohibition of figures, pictures or paintings in the Synagogue, exception has always been made in the case of the two carved or painted figures of two lions above the Ark holding the Ten Commandments. In some synagogues, deers are added, symbolizing the saying of the sages: "Be fleet as a hart and strong as a lion to do the will of thy Father who is in heaven." (Aboth V:23). Before the open face of the Ark, is suspended a silk or velvet curtain called *Parocheth,* overhung by a short drape. This is a reminder of the Tabernacle and the Temple. The *Parocheth* was the Temple curtain separating the holy space from the Holy of Holies (Ex. 26:31-34, Babli Kethuboth 106a). In many Portuguese synagogues there is no *Parocheth.* On the High Holidays special hangings of white silk are used, symbolizing forgiveness. The covers on the prayer desk and reading desk are likewise white. The curtains and covers are usually donations of women, who frequently embroider them with such designs as the Ten Commandments, the letters כ ת (the Crown of the Torah) with two lions holding a crown, and with their own names in Hebrew characters. The Ark is considered the holiest part of the Synagogue, never to be profaned, even if no longer in use. Nevertheless in emergency cases such as the caring for orphans or the redeeming of captives, it is permissible to sell even the Ark.

The *Ner Tamid* (Perpetual Light) is suspended above and in front of the Ark. It is one of the ancient ceremonials traceable to Biblical sources. In Exodus 27:20-21 and again in Leviticus 24:2 we read: "Command the children of Israel, that they bring unto thee pure olive oil beaten for the light, to cause a lamp to burn continually . . . . before the Lord." In the Temple in Jerusalem this light burned continually. Transferred into the Synagogue, it was interpreted as a symbol of the perpetual light contained in the Torah, for in the Torah's doctrine lies the Jew's way of life: in its study, his noblest delight. Thus the *Ner Tamid* is the true beacon of Israel's path. In the Synagogue, vacant or occupied, day or night, through the centuries, it creates an atmosphere of eternity, of faith, of hope, of the continuity of our people

INTERIOR OF SEPHARDIC SYNAGOGUE AT AMSTERDAM

and the timelessness of God. Delightful artistic forms have been given it. From wrought metal chains is usually suspended the bowl which originally was the receptacle for the oil to feed the flame. Oil has given way to gas and then to electricity; but the grace of the oil bowl still supports the light.

*Menorah.* At the right of the Ark, is placed the *Menorah,* the eight branched Chanukah lamp. In some synagogues the Ark is ornamented with the seven branched *Menorah* in the ancient form which it had in the sanctuary in Jerusalem, described in Exodus 25:31-40, and pictured on the Arch of Titus in Rome.

*Sefer Torah* (The Book of Teaching). The scroll kept in the Ark, contains the Five Books of Moses. For its ceremonial use in the Synagogue, it is never printed, never inscribed on paper, nor bound. Its form and its manner of

85

preparation are minutely prescribed in Jewish law and consecrated by uninterrupted practice from Bible times to our own day.

Parchment sheets—skins of ritually clean animals only—

THE TORAH
(H. U. C. Library)

cut to regulated sizes and set together in a specified way, form the very long sheet on one side of which is inscribed the whole of the Torah. The two ends of this sheet of parchment are attached to two rollers on either end of which are flat discs of wood topped by long handles. On these rollers (each called an *Etz chayim*, tree of life), the parchment is turned until the whole sheet is wound and the two rolls

meet. The discs at the ends keep the rolls straight and pro-
tected. On them and the handles, Biblical phrases and the
name of the donor are frequently carved or inlaid.

In Ashkenazic custom the rolled Torah is held together
by a *Mappa,* a silk or velvet band,
bound about it and tied or clasped.
A fitted embroidered velvet mantle of
purple, blue, or red (white for High
Holidays) is drawn over the top handles; and resting on the top discs, covers the parchment scroll. Hung from
the handles over the front of the mantle, is the *Tzitz* or breastplate. It is of
beaten silver or gold, formed with a
small pocket space to contain inserts
inscribed with the word Sabbath or
the names of other sacred days.

Suspended by a silver chain, hangs
the *Yod,* the pointer, the end of which
is formed like a small hand with an
extended index finger. This is employed by the person reading the Torah. The dressed Torah is topped by
either one broad *Kether* (crown) sit-
ting over the two long handles, or a

TORAH WITH
ORNAMENTS

smaller one for each handle. These crowns are usually elaborately formed of silver, and often adorned with tiny silver
bells.

Sephardic and Oriental Jews wrap the entire length of the
scroll with silk; and, instead of enclosing it in a mantle, lay
it into a *Tek,* a wooden box covered with silk or velvet.

The Torah is written in the square Hebrew letters with-

87

THE TORAH-SCRIBE

*Josef Israels*

out vocalization. For certain of these, there are prescribed embellishments called crowns, (*Ketharim*), crownlets or horns (*Taggin*). Spaces between letters, words, and lines; paragraphs and book divisions; spacing of texts, and other multiple details are all definitely regulated. The task of

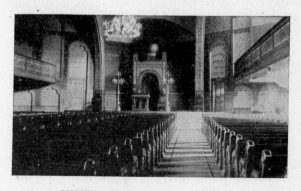

MODERN AMERICAN REFORM SYNAGOGUE

writing a scroll is an especially consecrated one; and the Jewish sages emphasize that the *Sofer* (*scribe*) must not only know and follow the regulations for the writing of each letter, but must be clean of hand and thought and filled with devotion to God.

*Organ and Choir Loft.* Since 1810 the Reform Synagogue has used the pipe organ in all religious services. This is built into either the rear of the synagogue auditorium in the balcony, or in the front above the Ark. According to its placement, the choir loft is set.

# IV

## PRAYER AND SONG

*Israel's prayers have ever been rendered in music. His liturgy evolved a distinctive musical calendar—a colorful expression of the significant dates in the Jewish year.*

# PRAYER AND SONG

THE prayer-books of the Jews are many and varied.
Different groups long widely divided geographically,
and different parties with divergent doctrines have, in the
course of time evolved rituals of their own. But beneath all
the variations, the framework of the Jewish service remains
the same—essentially patterned after the schedule of worship
in the Temple in Jerusalem. On this one framework is built
every service of the Jewish calendar.

The times of daily worship correspond to the times of the
ancient Temple services: Morning service—*Shacharith;* Afternoon service—*Mincha;* an Additional service for Sabbaths
and festivals—*Musaf.* Later there was instituted the Evening
service—*Maariv.*

The framework of the service is built upon seven chief
divisions:

FIRST are the Introductory Blessings.

SECOND are the Verses of Praise—*Pesuke dezimrah*—varied
and expanded for special days.

THIRD is the fundamentally important *Shema* with its
preceding and succeeding paragraphs.

THE FOURTH SECTION, adjusted and reshaped for different
services, but always present, is the Prayer—*Tefillah.* It is
called also *Amida,* which name refers to the practice of reciting it standing. (Most Reform congregations do not observe this custom.) This fourth section is further known as
the *Shemone esre* (Eighteen Benedictions). It retains this
name even when, as in certain services, it contains but seven

of its benedictions. Within this part of the service comes the Sanctification—*Kedusha.*

THE FIFTH DIVISION is Supplication—*Tachanun.*

SIXTH is the Reading of the *Torah* which occurs in certain morning and afternoon services.

THE SEVENTH DIVISION is the conclusion, containing the Adoration—*Olenu,* and the *Kaddish,* an exalted expression of the holiness of God.

Moreover, the pivotal prayers are permanent throughout the year's ritual. For example, the vital paragraphs of the *Shema* are repeated without change; certain of the benedictions of the *Tefillah* never fall out and never vary their text; and so on in each division of the service.

Within the established framework and around the permanent texts, special prayers are inserted, some omitted, and changes made in others, marking the differences between the services of the week-days, Sabbaths, festivals, fasts, and Holy Days.

Modern parties in Israel have added to the Hebrew prayer-book, translations of many of its prayers, and have eliminated much Medieval poetry which protracted the service. Reform Judaism has omitted the Additional service—*Musaf*—for Sabbaths and festal days. It has abbreviated to avoid repetitions and has rephrased many traditional prayers to escape outgrown attitudes and beliefs and to bring the ritual into closer conformity with the thinking of the modern enlightened Jew. But the chief prayers and the general outline of the service remain the same.

Alongside this strict adherence to the structure and essential texts, run two practices which prevent monotony and provide the distinctive coloring of the services of the different occasions. One is the varying of the texts of certain prayers and the insertion of special ones for each occasion of the religious calendar. The second one is singing.

Jewish prayer has ever been rendered in music. Since the institution of the Synagogue arose, the *chazzan* has chanted and sung, and the united voice of the congregation has responded. Given modes and tunes have been distinctive of certain seasons, of special days and events. This association of tune and service has created the coloring of the Jewish musical calendar. The same words of the same prayer in its same place in the service, when rendered in one musical mode instead of another, at once expresses the occasion, and determines the spirit and color of the service. The temporary musical chaos in the present day Synagogue, especially in the Western World, will surely not dam this stream of meaningful song!

The flavor of the Sabbath chant (*Shabbas nigun*) creates for the worshipper the atmosphere of the Sabbath (see pages 5-11). In the simplest purest form of this Sabbath mode, we present a selection of the Friday Evening Service: *Veshomeru,* page 100.

Unique in the music of the world is that of the Jews for the High Holy Days (see pages 12-21). Many of the prayers that we have pronounced all year, we repeat on these days. But so changed is the vehicle of their expression, so different the atmosphere created, that the very words carry new meaning and fresh spirit. The simpler familiar phrases of the daily service, which take on warmth and added beauty for the Sabbath, now sound forth with majesty and exaltation. The entire ritual of the High Holy Days is voiced in song of sustained grandeur. Therefore, while numerous chants and songs for these days are creations of compelling devotional beauty, the full glory of the music can be experienced only

95

in the completeness of the service that it interprets. Especially distinctive of *Rosh Hashanah* is the music of the *Shofar* service (see "Jewish Song Book," pages 204-207). Expressive of the spirit of the New Year is the hymn On Mighty Wings (see "Jewish Song Book," page 185). We select from the song of the service just one prayer text, for presentation here. Even a few bars of the traditional *Ovos* must carry the Jew, in thought, into the crowded Synagogue, and wrap him in the hushed awe of that sacred service. (*Ovos,* page 102.)

Beloved among the great melodies of *Yom Kippur,* and most famous in the world at large, is *Kol nidre.* Because of the general familiarity with this extraordinary number, we give only reference to the place where it may be found: "Jewish Song Book" English text, p. 215; with a Hebrew text, p. 252. A noble reworking in English of the Hebrew *Yaale* gives us the hymn so appropriate to the spirit of the day; "Jewish Song Book," p. 223. For its flexible beauty and its tone of awe, nothing surpasses the music to which is pronounced the description of the priests in the Temple in Jerusalem on the solemn Day of Atonement: *Vehakohanim,* page 106. At once awesome and joyous, the music of *Neilah* (the concluding service of *Yom Kippur*) accords with the sublimity of the prayers that it interprets. ("Jewish Song Book," pp. 245-251). It breathes the sweetness of human and divine reconciliation when, after the long hours of heart searching, the sun calmly sets on chastened spirits.

The characteristic tune of *Succoth* (see pages 22-26) is the *Lulav* melody which, in its association and rhythm, speaks the waving of the palm branches. To it, is set the festival response: *Hodu,* page 108.

From the ritual of *Simchath Torah,* we select music for the outstanding feature of the day's service: the processional about the Synagogue with the *Torah* Scrolls, expressive of Israel's joyous gratitude for receiving the Law. (See pages 26-27.) (*Onnoh,* page 109.)

To the Jews of Western Europe and America, the tune associated with *Chanukah* (see pp. 29-33) is: *Mooz Tzur*— Rock of Ages, page 110. Special insertions in the prayers of the regular services occurring during the eight days of the Feast of Lights, mark this celebration. For the chanting of the blessings, for the kindling of the *Chanukah* lights, see the "Jewish Song Book," page 115.

The half holiday of *Purim* (see pp. 34-37) brings into the Old Synagogue and into many private homes, the chanting of the *Megillah*. Many unique musical phrases have grown into this colorful chant. *Purim's* spirit of jollification, of gift-giving, masking, dancing, and the enjoying of special dainties, finds expression in the light-hearted Purim Song, p. 112.

For the *Pesach* Synagogue services, the music is that of the Three Festivals (*Succoth, Pesach, Shabuoth*), with the addition in Western Europe and America, of the melody distinctly associated with Passover: *Addir hu*—God of Might, page 114. Some of the loveliest music of *Pesach* (see pp. 38-44) is that for the *Seder* ("Jewish Song Book," pages 149, 150, 152, 154, 172-4).

*Shabuoth* (see pp. 47-48) interprets its service through the music of the Three Festivals. It adds the *Akdomus* tune. This is derived from the Psalm mode which may date back as far as Temple times. It is one of the oldest tunes that we have. We give the arrangement of it for the processional of the Confirmants: *Boruch haboh,* page 115. Well suited hymns for the day are Covenant of Sinai, "Jewish Song Book," p. 164, Confirmation Hymn, "Jewish Song Book," p. 264, and Consecration, p. 166.

## MINYAN

An ancient custom in Israel requires a quorum of ten adult Jews (see *Bar Mitzvah*) for public worship. In the Reform Synagogue, women too are counted to the *Minyan*.

THE FIRST PRINTED JEWISH MUSIC
from *Jewish Music* by Idelsohn

# Music

# Veshomeru

**Based on Adonoy Moloch mode**
**A. Z. IDELSOHN**

Ve - sho - me - ru    ve - ne yis - ro - el    es ha - sha -
bos,    la - a - sos es ha - sha - bos    le -
do - ro - som    be - ris    o-

lom. be - ni u - ven be - ne yis - ro-

el os hi le o - lom.

# Boruch
## (Ovos)

Traditional
accord. to arr. of S. Naumbourg

Bo - ruch  at - toh a - do - noy,  e - lo -
he - nu ve - lo - he.... a - vo - se - nu,  e -
lo - he av - ro - hom,  e - lo - he yitz- -

chok    ve - lo - he....    ya - a - -

kov.    ho - el....    ha - go - dol....    ha - gi -

bor ve - ha - no - roh,    el....    el - yon,    go -

mel cha-so-dim to - - vim ve-ko-ne ha-

kol ve - zo - cher chas-de o - vos, ve-zo-

cher.... chas - de............ o - -

vos,  u-me-vi *R. R. ge-u - loh  liv - ne...... ve-ne
             O. R. go - el

hem        le - ma - - - -

an   she-mo, le-ma-an sh'mo   be - a - ha - voh.

*R. R. Reform Ritual   O. R. Orthodox Ritual

# Vehakohanim

**Traditional**

*Moderato con moto*

1. Ve - ha - ko - ha-nim    ve - ho - om........    ho-
2. Me - fo - rosh    yo - tze........    mi-
3.     Ho - yu   ikor - im    u-

om - dim bo - a - - zo - roh, ke - she-
pi    ko - hen   go - dol, bi - ke-
- -mish - ta - - cha - vim u - mish-

*rall. . . .*

ho - yu shom - im es ha - shem,
du - - shoh bik - du - shoh uv - to - ho - roh,
ta - cha - vim ho - yu ko - re - im,

# Hodu

(for Succos)

Traditional

Ho - du la - do - noy
yo - mar noh

ki tov, ki lᵊ-o-
yis - - ro - el ki le-o-

lom— chas - do. yo - mar noh
lom— chas - do. yom - ru noh yir-

ves a - ha - ron ki le - o - lom chas - do.
e a - do - noy ki le - o - lom chas - do.

108

## Onnoh

**(during the procession)**

1. O - noh a - do - noy   ho - shi - oh noh,   o - noh a-
2. Elo - he ho - ru - chos   ho - shi - oh noh,   bo- chen le-
3. Zach ve - yo - shor   ho - shi - oh noh   cho - mel
4. Yode - ah macha - sho - vos   ho - shi - oh noh   ka - bir ve -

do - noy   hatz - li - choh   noh,   o - noh a - do-
vo - vos   hatz - li - choh   noh,   go - el cho-
da - lim   hatz - li - choh   noh,   tov   u - me-
no - or   hatz - li - choh   noh,   lo - vesh tze - do-

noy a - ne - nu   ve - yom kor - e - nu.
zok a - ne - nu   ve - yom kor - e - nu.
tiv a - ne - nu   ve - yom kor - e - nu.
kos a - ne - nu   ve - yom kor - e - nu.

# Rock of Ages

### Chanukah Hymn

Translated from the German
of Leopold Stein by M. Jastrow
and G. Gottheil

Traditional

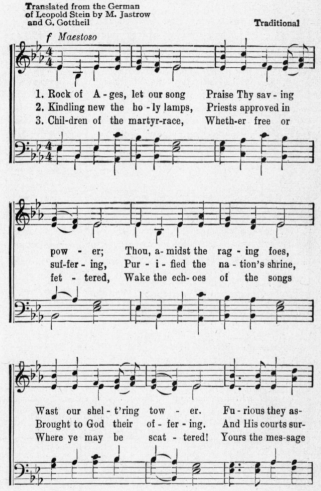

1. Rock of A - ges, let our song    Praise Thy sav - ing
2. Kindling new the ho - ly lamps,    Priests approved in
3. Chil-dren of the martyr-race,    Wheth-er free or

pow - er;    Thou, a- midst the rag - ing foes,
suf-fer - ing,    Pur - i - fied the na - tion's shrine,
fet - tered,    Wake the ech- oes of the songs

Wast our shel - t'ring tow - er.    Fu - rious they as-
Brought to God their of - fer - ing.    And His courts sur-
Where ye may be scat - tered!    Yours the mes-sage

110

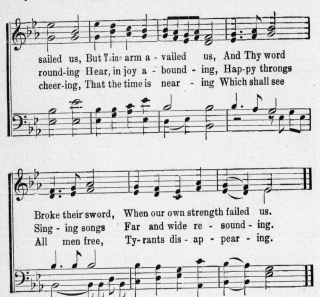

sailed us, But Thine arm a - vailed us, And Thy word
round-ing Hear, in joy a - bound - ing, Hap-py throngs
cheer-ing, That the time is near - ing Which shall see

Broke their sword, When our own strength failed us.
Sing - ing songs Far and wide re - sound - ing.
All men free, Ty - rants dis - ap - pear - ing.

# Purim Song

Based on Chassidic Motives
A. Z. IDELSOHN

A. IRMA COHON

*Allegro mf*

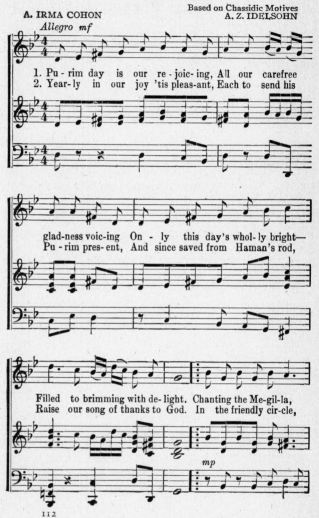

1. Pu - rim day is our re - joic - ing, All our carefree
2. Year - ly in our joy 'tis pleas-ant, Each to send his

glad-ness voic-ing On - ly this day's whol- ly bright—
Pu - rim pres- ent, And since saved from Haman's rod,

Filled to brimming with de-light. Chanting the Me-gil-la,
Raise our song of thanks to God. In the friendly cir-cle,

*mp*

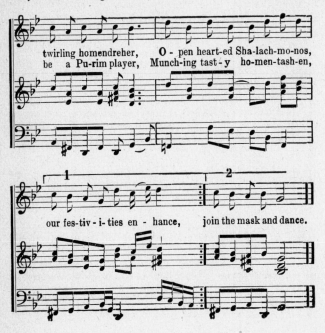

twirling homendreher,   O - pen heart-ed Sha-lach-mo-nos,
be   a Pu-rim player,   Munch-ing tast - y  ho-men-tash-en,

our fes-tiv - i- ties en - hance,   join the mask and dance.

# Addir hu—God of Might

English by G. Gottheil

Traditional

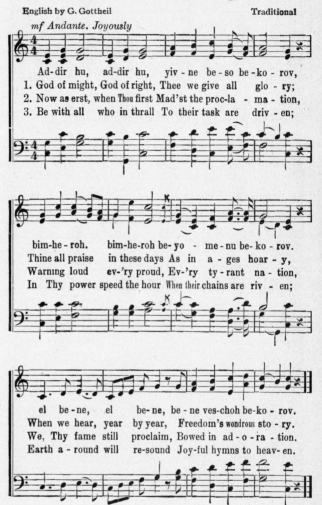

*mf Andante. Joyously*

Ad-dir hu, ad-dir hu, yiv-ne be-so be-ko-rov,
1. God of might, God of right, Thee we give all glo-ry;
2. Now as erst, when Thou first Mad'st the proc-la-ma-tion,
3. Be with all who in thrall To their task are driv-en;

bim-he-roh. bim-he-roh be-yo-me-nu be-ko-rov.
Thine all praise in these days As in a-ges hoar-y,
Warning loud ev-'ry proud, Ev-'ry ty-rant na-tion,
In Thy power speed the hour When their chains are riv-en;

el be-ne, el be-ne, be-ne ves-choh be-ko-rov.
When we hear, year by year, Freedom's wondrous sto-ry.
We, Thy fame still proclaim, Bowed in ad-o-ra-tion.
Earth a-round will re-sound Joy-ful hymns to heav-en.

## Boruch haboh

(For confirmation)

Utilizing traditional mode
A. Z. IDELSOHN

Bo-ruch ha-boh be-shem a-do-noy be-rach-nu-chem mi-bes a-do-noy, e-li a-toh ve-o - de-koh, e-lo-hay a-ro - me-me - koh. ho-du la-do-noy ki tov, ki le-o-lom cha - se-do. ki le-o-lom cha - se-do.

# V

# CEREMONIES
## FOR SPECIAL OCCASIONS

*Just as week-days and festivals are spiced
with ceremonies (which are symbols of
ideals), so also are special events in
the life of the Jew.*

# Brith Milah

THE Jewish boy is brought into a covenant with God, through the ceremony of circumcision (*Brith Milah*). Genesis 17 relates that our Patriarch Abraham first conceived of circumcision as a covenant of himself and his children with their God. The custom was known to the ancient world long before Abraham; but Abraham, in adopting it, interpreted it as a sign of a divine covenant. The custom did not immediately become firmly established in Israel. In Joshua 5:2-9, we read that in the time of Israel's sojourn in the desert, no circumcision was performed. Yet during the following centuries, the rite became so deeply rooted in Jewish tradition that, when Antiochus Epiphanes issued the prohibition against it (see Chanukah), Jews preferred to die rather than neglect it. It came to be the first condition made of any male proselyte to Judaism.

According to Jewish law, it is with the father or mother that the obligation rests, to have the boy circumcised. In the case of an orphan, the duty to provide for the rite, is the rabbi's. Without the consent of the mother, the father has no right to order the circumcision of his son. In case of the loss of two sons of the same mother, through circumcision, the third boy is exempt from the ceremonial obligation, because of the probability that the children of the given woman are hereditarily physically unfitted for the operation. A boy must be circumcised on the eighth day after birth, even though that day be a Sabbath or the Day of Atonement.

No postponement is permissible except for the illness of child or mother.

The night prior to the day of the *Brith Milah,* is called *Shalom Zachor* (Peace to the Boy). It was customary for a number of people to assemble to recite Psalms and sing special songs.

The *Brith Milah* is usually performed in the morning; and, if possible, in the presence of the required quorum of ten men (*Minyan*). At the celebration, the child is handed over from the mother to a man who carries the infant to the room where the ceremony is performed. This person is called "god-father" (in German *Gott-Vater*) which name in Yiddish, became *Kwater.* The man who is honored with the privilege of holding the child during the operation is known as *Sandik* (from the Greek syndikos—counsel). In the old communities, before the ceremony is performed, the child is laid upon the "Chair of Elijah," a special chair owned by the Synagogue and brought from there for the occasion. This custom is based upon a legend that the Prophet Elijah once complained to God that Israel was neglecting His covenant (1 Kings 19:10-14). In consequence of this accusation, God ordered him to be present at each circumcision, that he may witness Israel's loyalty to this covenant.

The operator is called by the Hebrew term *Mohel.* In times past he was generally a prominent member of the congregation who considered it a great privilege to introduce Jewish children into the sacred covenant. The average *Mohel* is so expert in this operation that no surgeon can compete with him in the dexterity of performance or in the safe-guarding of the life and health of the baby. A prominent surgeon is responsible for the statement that the instruments as well as the method traditionally employed, surpass those of the surgeon's. The "shield" which prevents the possibility of cutting into the flesh and which has no counterpart in the apparatus of the surgeon is still errone-

CHAIR OF ELIJAH (H. U. C. Museum)
Instruments of Circumcision
1. Knife          2. Shield          3. Sponge

ously looked upon by medical men as a ceremonial rather than as the most helpful and advanced means of protecting the child. It is still sold in Hebrew book stores and not in surgical supply houses. In the method of operating, the

*Mohel* is at an advantage, by reason of the swiftness with which the entire operation is performed (one cut instead of the usual three of the surgeon), because he makes no stitches, and causes a minimum loss of blood.

When the child is brought in, the assemblage arises and recites aloud several Biblical passages. The *Mohel* lays the child on the Elijah chair, chanting the while a prayer asking that his operation be successful, and concluding with the glorification of the ceremony. The child is laid either on a small operating table or on the lap of the *Sandik* who grasps the child's legs firmly. The *Mohel* recites a benediction reminding us of God's covenant with Abraham manifested through this rite. The father follows with a declaration to obey this command; and the assemblage responds: "Just as he is introduced into the covenant, so may he merit being introduced to *Torah,* marriage, and to good deeds." The operation and bandaging require hardly more time than do these benedictions. At the completion of his task, the *Mohel* recites the blessings over wine and concludes by announcing the child's name and by pronouncing a prayer for the baby and the hope that his parents may enjoy their child and may live to see him grown, a good Jew. Then the *Kwater* returns the infant to his mother.

Jewish art has found expression in the instruments of circumcision. The handle of the knife and the Elijah chair were elaborately carved.

In the Orient, it is customary that after the operation a banquet is served. In Europe a light repast is offered, partaking of which is considered a religious function.

# $\mathcal{M}$AZAL-TOV = good luck

UPON the birth of a child the stranger's question used to be "Is it a *Brith-Milah* or a *Mazal-tov?*" meaning: Is it a boy or a girl? On the first Sabbath after the girl's birth the father was called to the Synagogue platform during the reading of the *Torah*. The reader then announced the name of the child and concluded with a benediction for child and parents.

# $\mathcal{P}$IDYON $\mathcal{H}$ABBEN

THE "Redemption of the Son" is a ceremony for the first-born, if it be male. Among many ancient peoples the first-born of the mother, man or animal, was dedicated to the deity—either sacrificed or left at the sanctuary for sacred purposes (Exodus 13:2). Conditions modified the law by declaring (Exodus 13:12-13, Numbers 18:14-16) that the first-born of men be redeemed by the giving of a stipulated sum of money at the time when the boy is one month old. This is still practiced among Orthodox Jews, while Reform Judaism has discarded it. In case the parents are *Cohanim* (descendants of the priest tribe) the child is exempt from the need of redemption. The ceremony consists of the giving of five *shekalim* (now something like five dollars) to an Aaronite (a *Cohen*) who, in the presence of witnesses recites a prescribed ritual.

# *S*HIR *H*AMAALOS
## (or *Shir Hamaaloth*)

IMMEDIATELY after the birth of any child, the room in which the mother lay, used to be hung with placards inscribed with Psalm 121 and with cabalistic formulae against evil spirits. These placards took their name from the Psalm: *Shir Hamaalos (Hamaaloth)*.

SHIR HAMAALOS

# Bar Mitzvah

## (Son of Duty)

IN Jewish practice, a boy, to the age of thirteen, is considered a child. In times past, the father was—during those years of childhood—obliged to support him, to provide for his education, and to afford him the means of mastering a profession or trade. But at the age of thirteen the boy assumed religious duties and was considered an adult Jew (Aboth V:24). This change was symbolized by the son's putting on the *Tefillin* and in some congregations, also the *Tallith;* and by his being counted to a *Minyan*. (See page 98.)

At the present time and especially in Western countries, the *Bar Mitzvah* age no longer marks the end of childhood and of parental responsibility. The ceremony hence is entirely one for the strengthening of the boy's allegiance to his faith and his people, and for the encouraging of a mature attitude toward religious duties.

It is a great day in the life of a boy, on which he is introduced to his obligations as an adult Jew. The festivity is usually held on the Sabbath, even though the boy's birthday may have occurred during the week. In the Synagogue, the boy is called upon to pronounce the benediction over the Scripture. In the Orient and in Germany the boy reads from the Scroll either the entire portion of the week, or a paragraph of it, and concludes with the chanting of the *Haftarah* (the portion from the Prophets). In Eastern Europe the custom has been reduced to the chanting of the *Haftarah* only, while in American Synagogues the boys generally re-

*M. Oppenheim*

BAR MITZVAH

cite only the benedictions over the *Torah*. The purpose of the boy's public reading is two-fold: first to give proof of his knowledge of the *Torah,* and secondly to make him feel a full-fledged Jewish adult who, as such is entitled to conduct public service. After the readings, he is blessed with a special benediction, chanted by the chazzan or pronounced by the rabbi.

When the service is over, the event is celebrated by the parents at home. At the domestic gathering, in the presence of the guests, the boy sometimes used to hold a discourse, called *Derashah,* on a religious subject.

The *Bar Mitzvah* ceremony which is for boys only, is substituted in most Reform Jewish practice, by the Confirmation Service, obligatory for boys and girls alike. This service occurs but once a year, on *Shabuoth,* irrespective of the age of the confirmant.

# CHATHUNAH
## (*Wedding*)

THIS most important celebration in human life, the Jew has provided with many ceremonies. The most outstanding custom formerly preliminary to every Jewish wedding, is called *Baddekens*—the covering of the hair and face of the bride. It dates far back. There are still among us women wearing the *Sheitel* (see page 73).

On the day of the wedding until after the marriage ceremony, both bride and groom used to fast to atone for their sins.

Music making before and after the wedding ceremony has been customary from most ancient times. It was retained even after the destruction of the Second Temple, while other music was prohibited as a sign of mourning, for the rabbis considered it essential to a wedding. The music would start long before the ceremony, both in the house of the groom and in that of the bride, lasting until all the guests were gathered (the men in the groom's house, the women in the bride's). The music makers were as a rule Jewish instrumentalists (*Klezmer*). They would lead the procession to the *Chuppah* (the marriage canopy), which used to be erected in the open air in the court of the Synagogue. First, the groom was led in procession, accompanied by the father, male relatives and guests, then the bride, accompanied by the mother and the women present.

The canopy is a reminder of the ancient tent-life of Israel. Bedouin tribes to the present day erect a special tent for the young couple, in which the bridal bed is set. In the course of cultural development, when the Jewish people came to live in substantial buildings, the *Chuppah* was still retained, and a mystic significance read into it. It was supposed to symbolize the canopy made of the skin of the Leviathan (a mythical fish) in which the people expected to live in Paradise.

During the procession, the bystanders showered the young couple with raisins and almonds, or with rice. These showers signify the hope for happiness and productivity. When the bride reached the *Chuppah* she had to walk around the bridegroom three times. Many reasons are offered for these circuits. The simplest one is that the bridegroom might assure himself of the identification of his bride. As she took her place beside the groom, the couple was draped under one

*Jew. Encyc., Vol. VIII*

CHUPPAH (WEDDING CEREMONY)
Marriage Scene in Gallicia

*Tallith*. The parents, because they led the couple to the *Chuppah* (or in the case of orphans, other near relatives who assumed this role) were called *Unterführers* (those who lead in). The *Unterführers* stood at the *Chuppah* during the ceremony. Then the rabbi or any other respected and learned Jew would pronounce the "betrothal benediction" (*Birchath Erusin*) in the traditional chant. In

*Jew. Encyc., Vol. III*

ITALIAN KETHUBAH OR BETROTHAL DEED
—1795

places where the canopy is no longer accounted essential to the ceremony, often a floral canopy or arch is erected for beauty and as a link with the old custom of the *Chuppah*. In olden times, the ring was not known at all. Instead a coin was handed by the groom to the bride. This was a relic of the time when men bought their wives. The usage of the wedding ring was introduced in Israel as late as the eighth century C. E. Certain regulations were prescribed for the ring. It had to be smooth and round, with no marks and no stones. The bridegroom, when placing the ring on the bride's finger (formerly, the index finger of the right hand), said in Hebrew: *Hare at mekudesheth li betabaath zu kedath moshe*

WEDDING RINGS
Upper—15th and 16th Century
Lower—16th and 17th Century

*veyisrael* (Be consecrated unto me through this ring, according to the law of Moses and Israel). In Western Europe and America there is frequently an exchange of rings between bride and groom.

The marriage benedictions are then pronounced. The declaration of the groom and the "wedding blessings" (*Birchoth Nissuin*), called the "Seven Benedictions" (*Sheva berachoth*) still constitute the essentials of a Jewish wedding ceremony. One of these blessings is recited over a cup of wine out of which bride and groom drink. The rabbi would then read the marriage contract (*Kethubah*), in its original Aramaic wording. The use of this ancient "bill of rights" has been discarded by Reform Jews. A dish was then thrown at the feet of the bridegroom. He would step on it and crush it. This custom is of early origin, and is founded on various superstitious beliefs. Later it was re-interpreted as a reminder to the young people, at the climax of their joy, of the destruction of the Temple.

The couple was then led back in procession with musical accompaniment, to the house of the parents of either the groom or bride, where the banquet (*Seudah*) was served. The instrumentalists would usually choose more joyous tunes for the returning from the *Chuppah* than for the procession to it.

In olden times, and in the Orient to the present day, the banqueting continued for an entire week. At each meal, the "wedding benedictions" are chanted, and special wedding songs are sung. In many communities such as the Yemenite, Syrian and Eastern European, a rich treasury of wedding songs has been created in Hebrew as well as in the vernacular. At the meal, much stress was laid upon the twisted bread (*Challah*) and the soup called *"Goldene Youch."*

# Mourning

WHEN the Jew faces the closing moments of his life, he utters again the watchword of his faith. At that moment a relative or the rabbi recites with him, the *Shema* and the confession (*Viddui*).

Before the days of the present municipal supervision and efficient undertaking service, when the care of the dead was left to the family and friends, the Jews were scrupulous about respectful tending and disposal of the body. A so-called Holy Society (*Chevra Kadisha*) existed in every community throughout the ages. Membership in it was accounted a great merit. Its task consisted in caring for the dead body, arranging the funeral, and preparing the grave. In the Middle Ages often the members of the Society faced most dangerous situations in saving the bodies of Jews killed by Gentiles, and in bringing them to burial in a Jewish cemetery. Needless to say, the services of the *Chevra Kadisha* were performed without remuneration.

Immediately following death, the body was laid on the floor with a light at the head and one at the feet. Usually a member of the *Chevra Kadisha* kept watch until the funeral. The body was washed (Hebrew: *Tahara*) by the members of the Society and wrapped in a white shroud (Hebrew: *Tachrichim*). In many cases, a man preserved his *Kittl* to be wrapped in, also his *Tallith*. In some communities, it was customary to march about the corpse seven times (*Hakafoth*—encirclings) while reciting a ritual. Then the body was laid into a coffin or—in some countries, especially in the Orient—on a stretcher, and carried to the cemetery.

Before the medical testimony of death became a governmental order, it was customary to bury the body on the day of the death, and only in case the day happened to be Sabbath or a holiday, was the funeral postponed until the next day.

The grave, according to tradition, had to be dug in conformity with given measurements and with its head-end pointing eastwards toward Jerusalem. After the body was placed into the grave, three pieces of broken pottery were laid upon the eyes and mouth, symbolizing the vanity of the eyes and mouth. A handful of Palestinian earth was laid under the head. The close relatives, at the open grave, tore their garments over the heart (to the width of four fingers (Hebrew: *Keria*) as a sign of sorrow.

As soon as the grave is closed, Kaddish is recited by the close relatives. This recitation the mourners repeat for eleven months at every public service. In addition a ritual is recited and the prayer for the soul of the departed (*El mole rachamim*) is chanted by the *Chazzan* or any other man present.

From the grave, the mourners (Hebrew: *Avelim*) return home where they are obliged to remain seven days, to sit on the floor and to walk without shoes, as signs of mourning customary in ancient Israel. During these seven days (Hebrew: *Shiva*), public services are held at the house of the departed one, and only on Sabbath the mourners go to the Synagogue. There, after the chanting of *Lecha dodi,* the *Chazzan,* accompanied by the rabbi meets the mourners at the entrance of the Synagogue, saying: "May God comfort you together with the mourners of Zion." During the eleven months, the mourners are expected to be mindful of their loss and to conduct themselves accordingly.

In America, the regulations of the Board of Health and the equipment and service of the undertakers, leave to the family of the deceased only the providing of the burial place and the ritual of the interment. A short service is held at the home, if the body is brought back there from the embalmer's. Sometimes this service takes place at the chapel of the undertaker's or the chapel at the cemetery. In the case of a Synagogue funeral, the corpse is carried there for the service, and the ritual read in the synagogue. Sometimes—especially for a person of importance—a funeral address (*Hesped*) is delivered by the rabbi.

At the open grave a brief ritual is read. The coffin is lowered, the grave closed, and the *Kaddish* recited. Services are usually conducted at the mourner's home during the following few days—exclusive of Sabbaths and holidays.

As formerly, the mourners recite the *Kaddish* for a period of eleven months.

At the end of the first year, and on the same date of each succeeding year, the *Yahrzeit* (anniversary of the death) is observed, by reciting *Kaddish* at the public services in the Synagogue and by kindling a lamp or a candle—symbol of the soul of the deceased. It was customary to fast on the day of *Yahrzeit* and to give charity.

Shamah Yisrael addonai elohenu
addonai echod. — Deut. 6:4.